shorelines

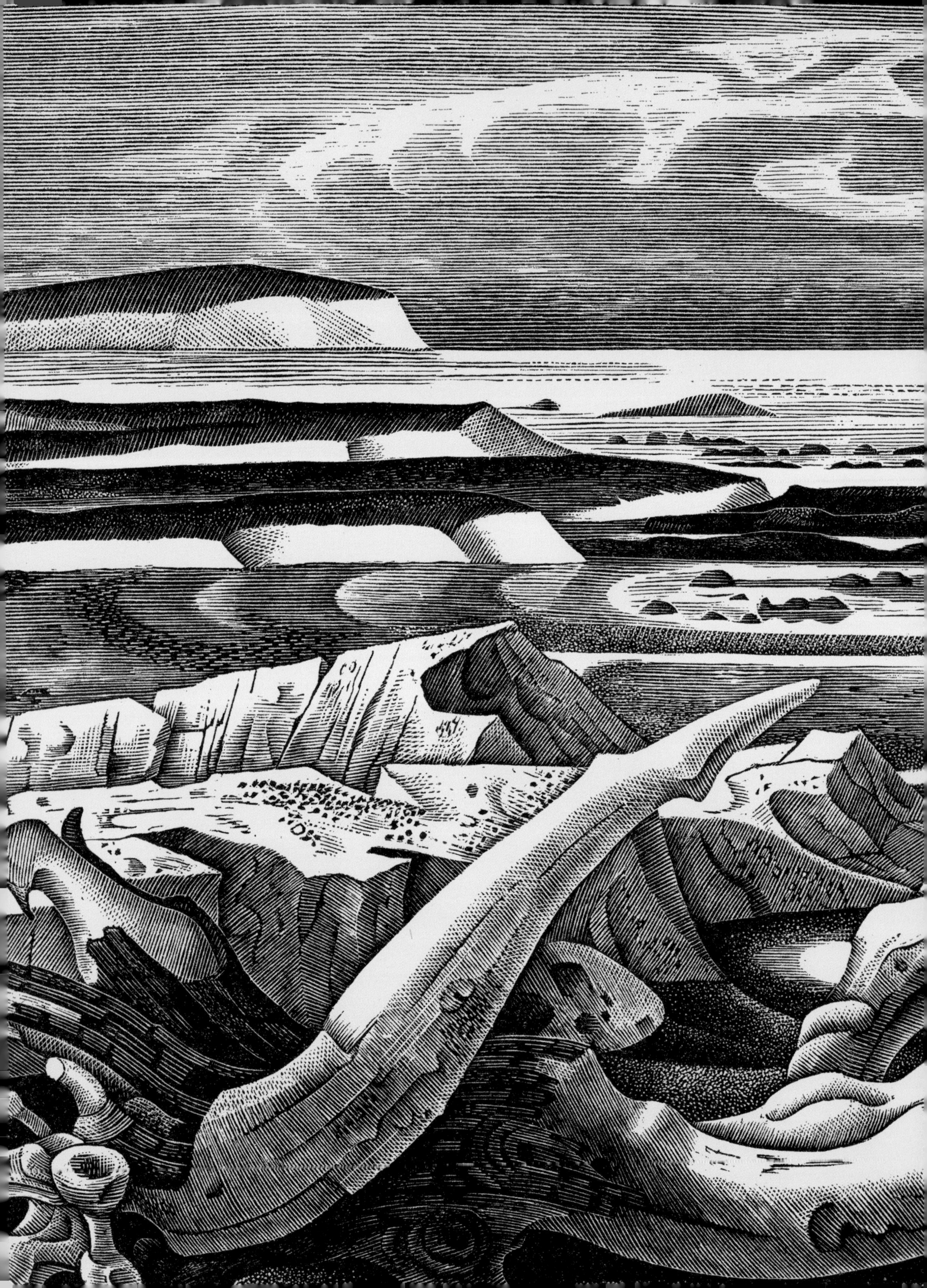

shorelines

artists on the south coast

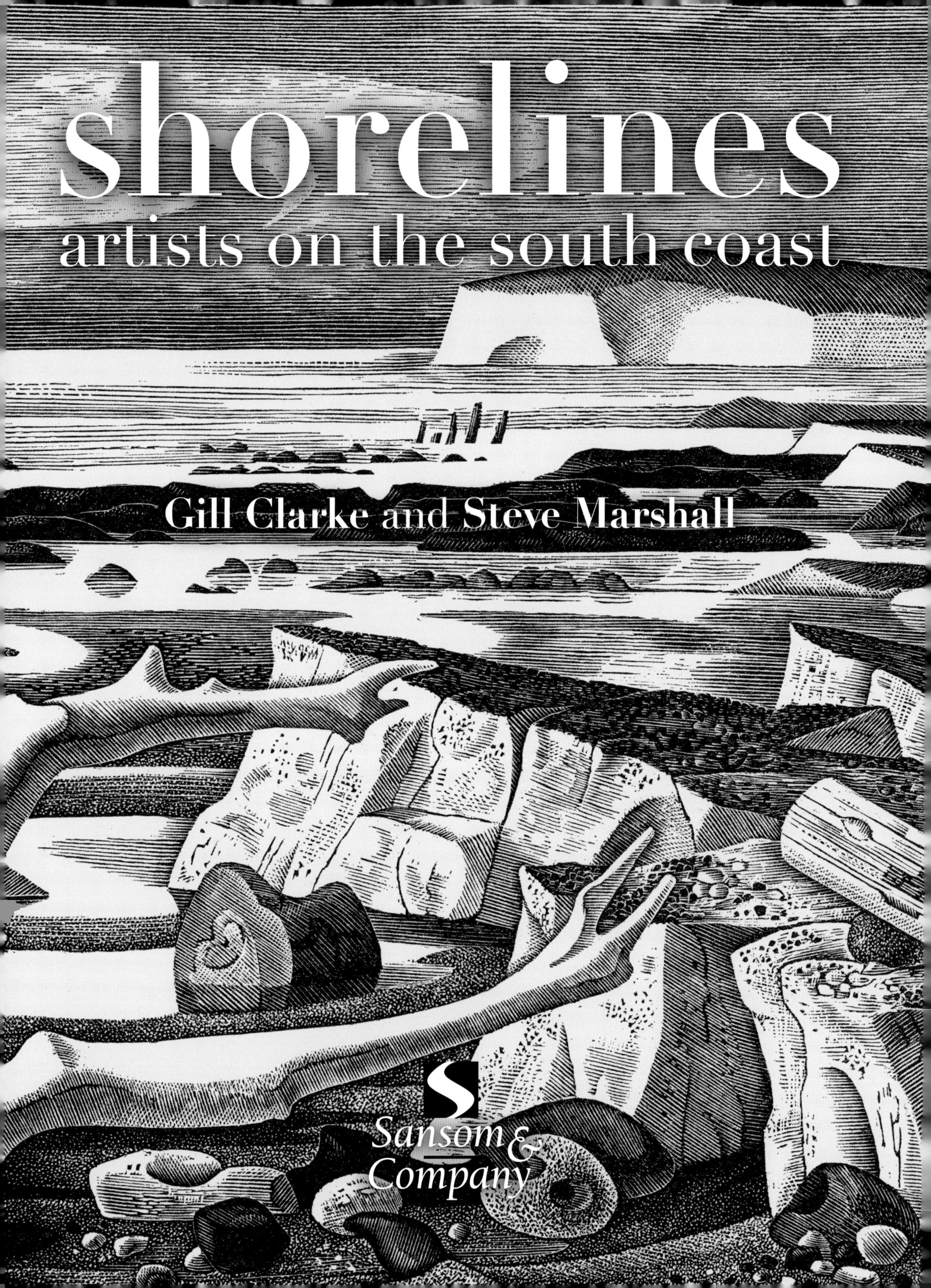

Gill Clarke and Steve Marshall

Sansom & Company

First published in 2015 by Sansom & Co.,
a publishing imprint of Redcliffe Press Ltd.,
81G Pembroke Road, Bristol BS8 3EA

www.sansomandcompany.co.uk
info@sansomandcompany.co.uk

Published to accompany the exhibition at:
St. Barbe Museum & Art Gallery, 19 September 2015–9 January 2016
(New Street, Lymington, Hampshire SO41 9BH | www.stbarbe-museum.org.uk)

ISBN 978-1-908326-76-8

British Library Cataloguing-in-Publication Data
A catalogue record for this book is available from the British Library

Design and typesetting by E&P Design
Printed and bound by Cambrian Printers Ltd

Front cover: Eric Ravilious, *Newhaven Harbour*, 1937, lithograph on paper, Victoria and Albert Museum
Rear cover: Jeremy Gardiner, *Durdle Door, Sunrise*, 2007, acrylic and jesmonite on panel, © Jeremy Gardiner
Frontispiece: Monica Poole, *Driftwood* (detail), 1979, wood engraving, Julian Francis Collection © Estate of the Artist

CONTENTS

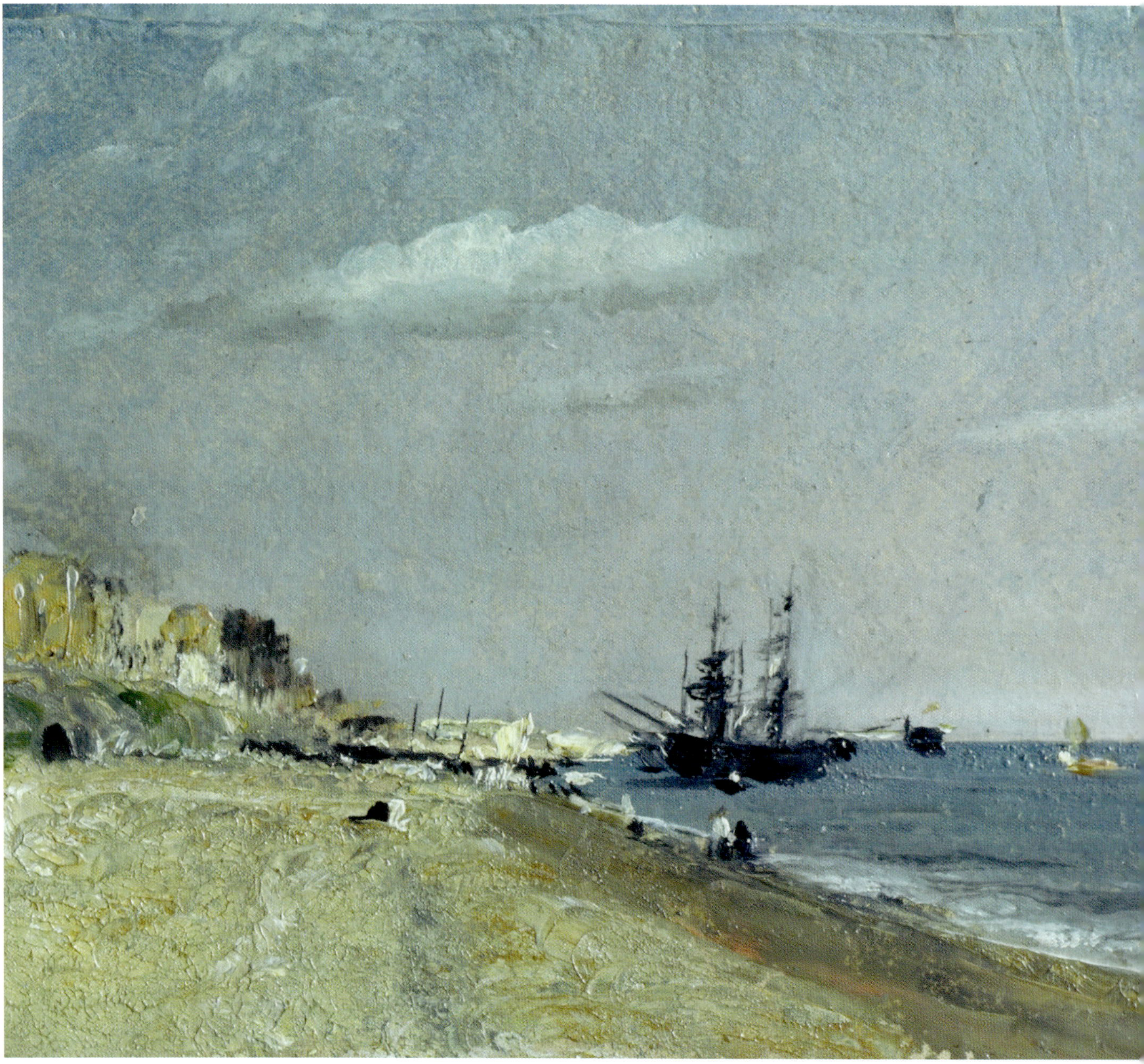

FOREWORD

ST. BARBE MUSEUM & ART GALLERY IS SITUATED IN LYMINGTON, a town which looks both north to the New Forest and south to the Solent. Over the years we have developed a number of exhibitions which have looked at artists' responses to these two very different landscapes – the woods and heathland of the Forest and the narrow stretch of water which was the birthplace of British yachting. Two years ago we broadened our northern horizon by tackling the subject of artists' treatment of trees in the exhibition 'Under the Greenwood: Picturing the British Tree from Constable to Kurt Jackson'. It was natural then to take the same approach to our south-facing aspect with this exhibition 'Shorelines: Artists on the South Coast'. From the Solent we have travelled east and west to examine the subjects and motivations that have brought artists to the south coast from the eighteenth century to the present. In the interests of relevance and manageability we have restricted the content to the Channel coast of which our local shoreline forms an important element. As it would be extremely difficult to make any examination of artists' views of Cornwall's southern coast without including St. Ives we have crept a little way on to that county's Atlantic coast.

As we developed the exhibition and selected works the wealth of material relating to this subject quickly became apparent. In reality we could have mounted separate exhibitions for each of the topics we have covered in outline here, and perhaps in due course we will. Our choice of works has been informed by the desire to highlight key themes but also to provide a fresh perspective by focusing on the natural and man-made landscape of the coast rather than the sea itself. We were also particularly keen to represent some neglected but significant artists and to include a range of media including oil paintings and watercolours, but also drawings and artist's printmaking processes such as wood engraving, lithography and etching. As a result iconic paintings by nationally renowned figures rub shoulders with works by lesser known artists and together these provide a diverse and stimulating interpretation of our southern coast.

We begin with an overview which highlights some of the fashions and cultural developments which have brought artists to the coast in general and the south coast in particular at different times. 'Storms and Safe Havens' explores the conflicting character of the coast as a place of refuge and calm and as an environment regularly battered by the fury of the elements. 'The Working

Coast' looks at the activities which have sustained coastal communities and supported Britain's development as a global maritime power: fishing, boat building, quarrying, trade and transport. 'Seaside Pleasures' charts the development of the south coast as a prime tourist destination from the days of the salt water cure to the packed beaches of the mid-twentieth century. In contrast 'Ruling the Waves' explores the Channel coast's role as frontier and fortress, encompassing Tudor castles, Napoleonic Martello towers, naval dockyards and the threat posed to this island nation by the rise of air power during the Second World War. Finally 'Strange Tides' visits the odd and uncanny representations of the southern shore made by artists who incorporated surrealism and abstraction in a new approach to landscape painting.

Gill Clarke and Steve Marshall
May 2015

pp. 6–7: John Constable's
Brighton Beach with Colliers (page 65)

ACKNOWLEDGEMENTS

WE WOULD LIKE TO THANK THE LENDERS WHO PROVIDED works for the exhibition: British Council, Government Art Collection, Imperial War Museum, Ingram Collection of Modern British and Contemporary Art,Isle of Wight Council Heritage Service, National Maritime Museum, Poole Museum Service, Portsmouth Museum Service, Russell-Cotes Art Gallery & Museum, Shell Art Collection, Southampton City Art Gallery, Towner, Eastbourne and Victoria and Albert Museum. At those institutions we would particularly like to thank: Diana Eccles at the British Council; Chantal Condron, Adrian George and Nicole Simoes da Silva at the Government Art Collection; Maria Rollo at the Imperial War Museum; Chris Ingram and Jo Baring at the Ingram Collection; John Fletcher at Isle of Wight Council Heritage Service; Sue Beckett at Poole Museum Service; Katy Ball at Portsmouth Museum Service, Sue Hayward and Duncan Walker at the Russell-Cotes Art Gallery and Museum; Emma Mackinnon at Shell Art Collection; Tim Craven at Southampton City Art Gallery; Karen Taylor at Towner, Eastbourne; Rebekka Deighton, Ruth Hibbard and Hannah Kauffman at the V&A.

We would also like to thank Jeremy Gardiner, Kurt Jackson, Francis Carline, Julian Francis and Stuart Southall and the owners of private collections who kindly loaned items for the exhibition.

For their help with images and copyright clearance for the catalogue Philippa Bambach and Caroline Toppin; Bridgeman Images; Jeffery Camp; Myrna Chave; DACS; The Fergusson Gallery, Perth and Kinross Council; John Croft and the Trustees of the Estate of Dame Laura Knight; David Joel; John Peel at Manchester Art Gallery; The Royal Collection; Tate Images; Laetitia Yhapp.

Such an ambitious exhibition project would not have been possible without the support and commitment of the Trustees and staff at St. Barbe Museum & Art Gallery. Our thanks in particular go to Mark Tomlinson, Director and Laura Bullivant, Community Engagement and Learning Officer (Hampshire Cultural Trust).

We would also like to thank the staff of Hampshire Libraries, particularly at Emsworth and Lymington, the London Library and the National Art Library. Thanks also to Sarah Gilroy and Amy Marshall. We are also grateful to Clara Hudson, John Sansom and Ian Parfitt for producing this book.

Finally we are extremely grateful to the sponsor for this exhibition: Rathbones Brothers plc.

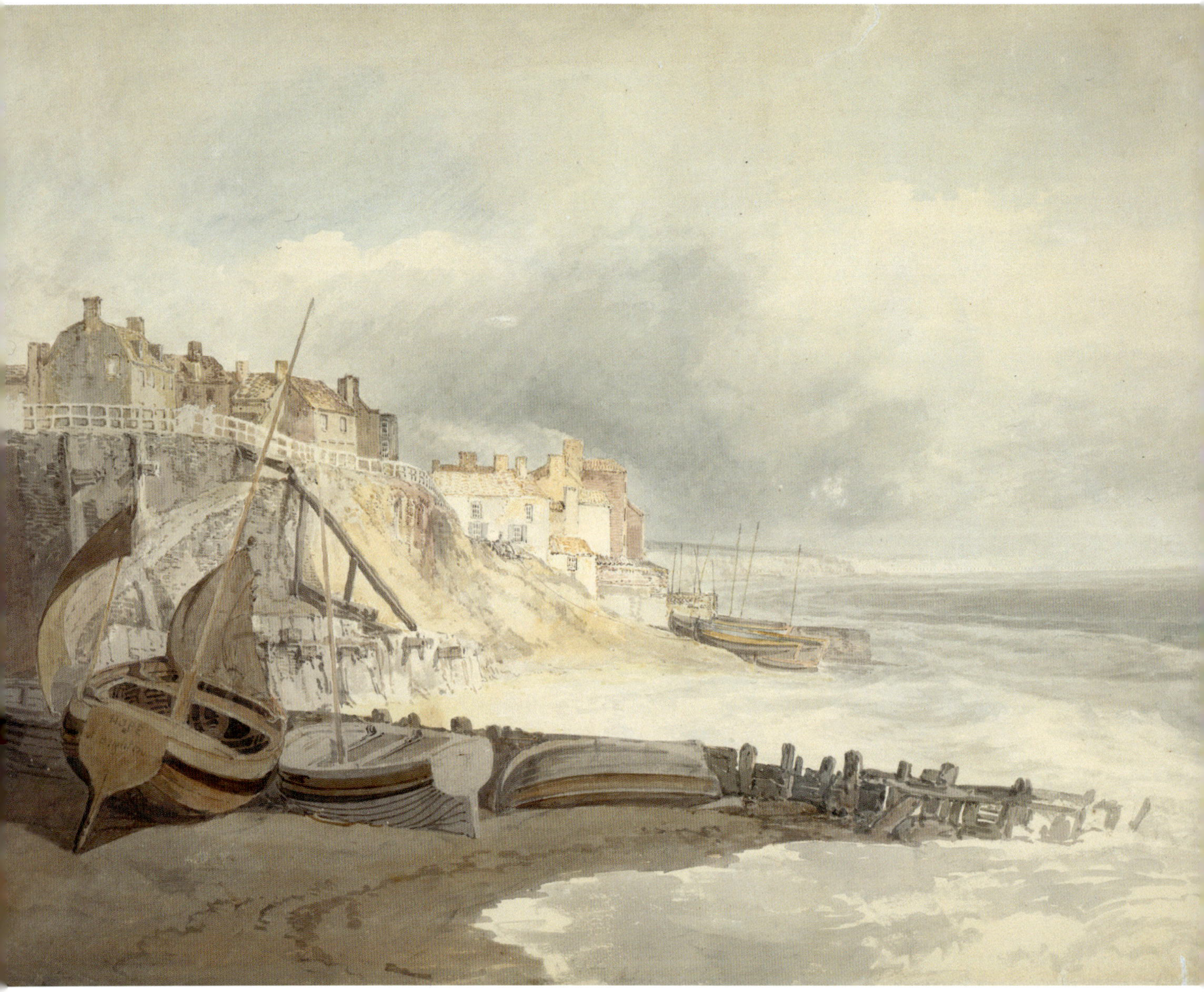

JMW TURNER
Brighthelmstone
c.1796 | watercolour | 413 x 548 mm
VICTORIA AND ALBERT MUSEUM

ARTISTS ON THE SOUTH COAST

STEVE MARSHALL

A TOUR OF THE COASTS OF HAMPSHIRE, SUSSEX AND KENT IN 1774 prompted William Gilpin, champion of the picturesque, to eulogise about the many attractions that an artist might find on these shores:

> In *coast scenery* … if its character be preserved distinct, the ideas of grandeur rise very high. Winding bays – views of the ocean – promontories – rocks of every kind and form – estuaries – mouths of rivers – islands – shooting peninsulas – extensive sandbanks; and all these adorned occasionally with castles – light-houses – distant towns – towers – harbours – all the furniture of navigation, and other incidental circumstances which belong to sea-coasts, form a rich collection of grand and picturesque materials.[1]

His checklist of rewarding subject matter neatly summarises the features which have attracted artists to the Channel coast over the last three hundred years. Their motivations varied: some came in search of fresh stimulus, some were hoping for drama, others sought escape from the city or the threat of war. Fashion has had its influence too, whether for picturesque tourism, a health-giving visit to a coastal resort or the cachet of a flourishing art colony. Artists might be inspired by a wartime commission from the government or the isolation in which to explore personal and sometimes esoteric visions. Whatever their purposes and preoccupations, all these artists shared one thing: the inspiration they drew from the southern shore.

The Channel coast runs for just over three hundred miles between Margate in Kent and Land's End in Cornwall. At its narrowest point just twenty-one miles separate the French mainland from Dover, England's traditional gateway to continental Europe. Invading armies from Rome and Normandy made the short trip across the Channel to write new chapters in British history. Missionaries, migrants and refugees landed here, bringing new cultures and ideas, and from the Channel's ports Britain's explorers, merchants and settlers have set out across the globe. The south coast is a dynamic environment in every sense, its geography in slow but continual flux and millions of years of history are revealed in the geological and fossil records of its clay and stone. Its complex geology has also provided a remarkably varied coastline of imposing cliffs, rocky bays, sand and shingle beaches, estuaries and salt marshes, features that have in turn shaped the distinctive histories of its coastal communities.

1. Gilpin, W. (1804), *Observations on the Coasts of Hampshire, Sussex, and Kent, relative chiefly to Picturesque Beauty, made in the summer of the year 1774*, Cadell and Davies, p.3.

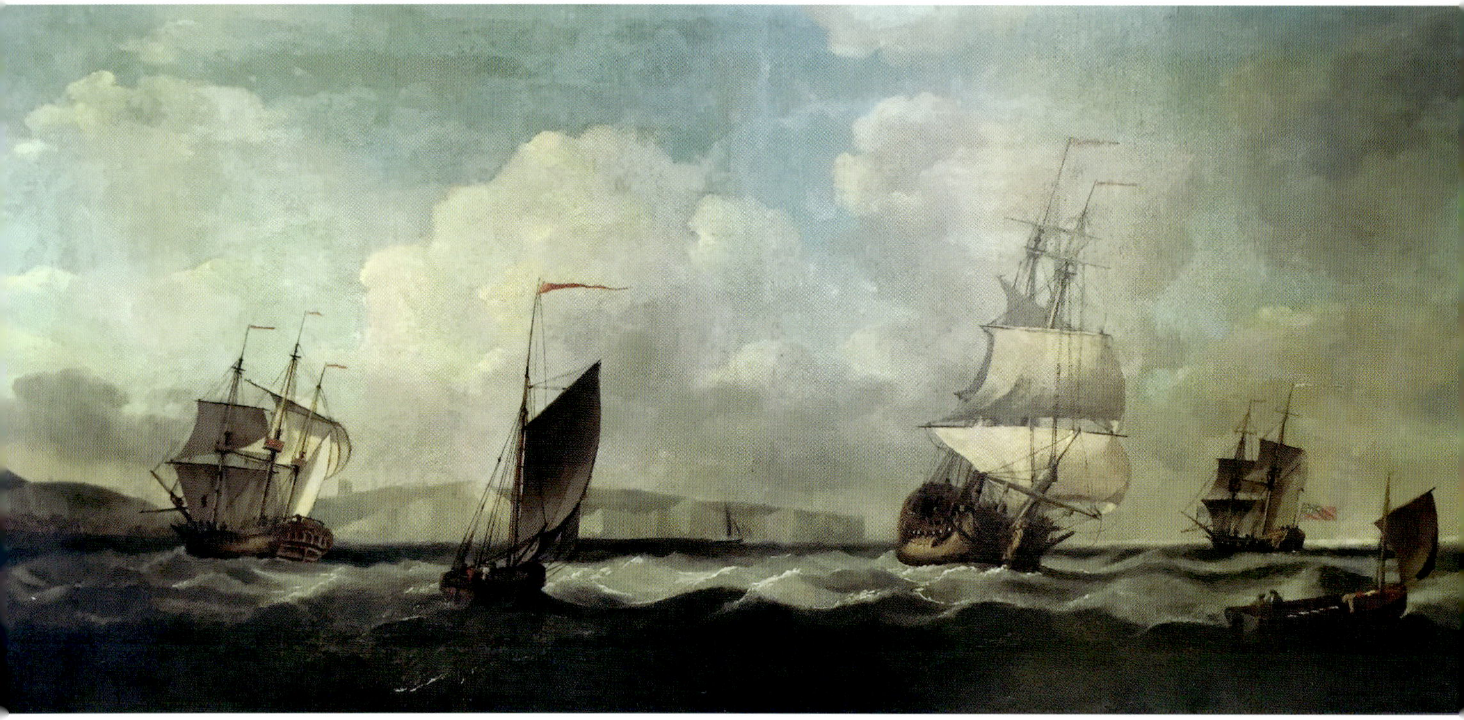

CHARLES BROOKING
Two English Frigates, a Brig and Other Sailing Vessels off Dover
oil on canvas | 550 x 1220 mm
PRIVATE COLLECTION

WHEN ARTISTS BEGAN ARRIVING ON THE SOUTH COAST IN THE early eighteenth century the attraction was not in the landscape of the shore but the fleets which were busily establishing Britain as the world's premier naval and trading power. The nation's identity and growing self-confidence were closely entwined with Britannia's rule over the waves and there was a market, particularly among the owners and captains of ships, for representations of heroic naval actions and the less glamorous but equally important work of the merchant fleet. In painting for this audience marine artists needed a thorough understanding of a ship's appearance in varying states of tide and wind and there was an emphasis on the accurate portrayal of hull, sail and rigging. Where coastal landscapes were included they were often merely a backdrop for the action of the ships upon the waves. Britain's fledgling marine painters were working within a tradition previously established by the Dutch, brought to England when Charles II invited the Van de Velde family to take up residence at Greenwich around 1672.[2] Perhaps the most accomplished artist of this generation was Charles Brooking (1723–59), who died tragically young and whose unique abilities are slowly gaining recognition. Andrew Graham-Dixon has championed his work, writing: 'Brooking captured the vivid, vaporous skies of the British coastline, full of wind and freshness and fast-moving clouds, with just as much skill and passion as John Constable would bring to the same subject matter half a century later.'[3] *Two English Frigates, a Brig and Other Sailing Vessels off Dover* (undated) with its formal title typical of the genre, can be read simply as a patriotic marine painting. In the distance stand the white cliffs with the keep of Dover Castle suggested above, symbolic of a proud and independent nation safe behind its island walls. Two frigates patrol the coastal waters, a reassuring presence for the merchant brig heading towards the harbour without fear of an enemy based but a few miles across the Channel. The ships are picked out in a pool of sunlight in contrast with the dark 'step' in the foreground, a device employed by the Dutch marine artists to draw the eye into the picture and give variety to the appearance of the waves.[4] The fact that three quarters of the canvas is given over to the sky is revealing of Brooking's growing interest in atmospheric effect. This focus is even more pronounced in his masterpiece *Ships in a Light Breeze* (undated), where the cloud patterns, weather conditions and play of light on water are given as much attention as the vessels.

From 1740 onwards Britain was almost constantly at war with France and the resulting difficulties in continental travel meant that the Grand Tour was effectively cancelled until further notice. Those seeking new vistas had to turn their gaze closer to home. At around the same time new theories on beauty, the sublime and the picturesque in art were being discussed and promoted and these helped to provide a solution for the would-be cultural traveller – the picturesque tour. The great populariser of these tours was the Reverend William Gilpin (1724–1804) who in 1768 defined picturesque as 'a term expressive of that peculiar kind of beauty, which is agreeable in a picture.'[5] He published a series of books which took the 'traveller with pencil' to the Wye valley, the Lake District, Scotland, the New Forest and the Isle of Wight. These illustrated guides identified suitably picturesque locations and instructed the visitor on how they might amend and embellish what nature had provided to create satisfying works of art.

In 1777 Gilpin had become the Vicar of Boldre, a village just outside Lymington, a few miles from the coast. It was natural that he should turn

2. Joel, D. and Taylor, J. (2000), 'Charles Brooking and the Dutch School of Marine Painting', in *Charles Brooking 1723–1759 and the 18th Century British Marine Painters*, Antique Collectors' Club, p.25.
3. Graham-Dixon,, A. (2009), 'The Call of the Sea', exhibition review in *The Sunday Telegraph*, 20 September 2009.
4. Joel, D. and Taylor, J. (2000) Op. cit., p.20.
5. Gilpin, W. (1802), *An Essay on Prints*, T. Cadell and W. Davies, p.xii.

his attention to the attractions of his adopted home in the book *Remarks on Forest Scenery* (1791). One of the tours included brings the picturesque traveller to the Solent shore:

> From the little peninsula, on which Hurst-castle stands, you are entertained with views on each hand. The island, and the Needle-rocks are objects, dreary, vast and grand; and not wholly unpicturesque. But to make them objects of the pencil, they must be well inlightened, and the fore-ground adorned with a little naval furniture – an anchor, a net hanging to dry, a drifted boat, or some other object, with which sea-coasts abound.[6]

Gilpin produced a pen and wash drawing *View of the Needles* (1791) which would be reproduced as an aquatint in the book. The painting does not follow his instructions to the letter, but you would be hard pressed to find the rocky outcrop in the foreground anywhere along this stretch of the coast; it is an artistic embellishment, added to frame the view and heighten the picturesque qualities of the scene. Gilpin's very specific and often pedantic instructions make for enjoyable reading but did lend themselves to satire. The success of his books and the resulting vogue for picturesque travel provided an obvious target and Gilpin was mercilessly lampooned by William Coombe (1742–1823) and Thomas Rowlandson (1756–1827) in *The Tour of Doctor Syntax in Search of the Picturesque* (1813):

> I'll make a TOUR – and then I'll WRITE IT.
> You well know what my pen can do,
> And I'll employ my pencil too:-
> I'll ride and write, and sketch and print,
> And thus create a real mint;
> I'll prose it here, I'll verse it there
> And picturesque it everywhere.[7]

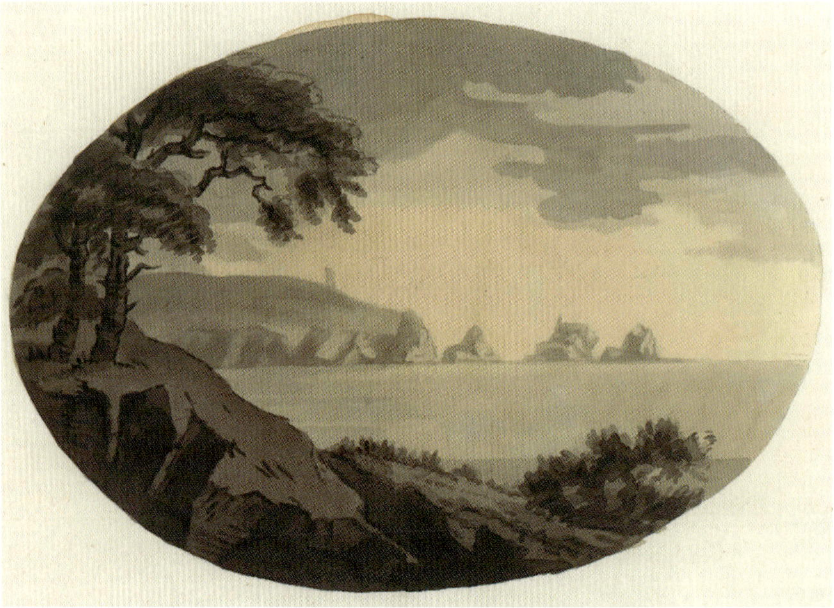

WILLIAM GILPIN
View of the Needles
1791 | pen and wash | 180 x 320 mm
PRIVATE COLLECTION

6. Gilpin, W. (1791), *Remarks on Forest Scenery and other Woodland Views, relative chiefly to Picturesque Beauty, illustrated by the Scenes of the New-Forest in Hampshire*, vol. II, R. Blamire, p.89.
7. Coombe, W. (1812), *The Tour of Doctor Syntax in Search of the Picturesque: A Poem*, reprinted by John Campbell, Philadelphia, 1865, p.17.

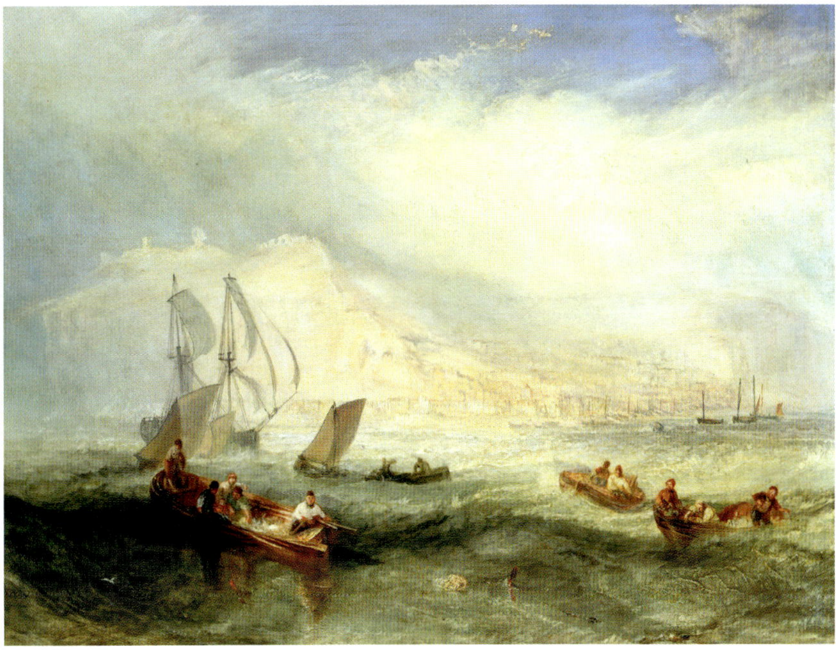

JMW TURNER
Line Fishing, off Hastings
c.1835 | oil on canvas | 584 x 762 mm
VICTORIA AND ALBERT MUSEUM

This is a little harsh, Gilpin certainly did not publish the tours to make money, indeed income from his writings and paintings helped to fund the school he established for the poor children of Boldre. There is also no denying his sincerity and perceptiveness in promoting the British landscape's qualities to artists both amateur and professional.

WHEN THE 1774 TOUR BROUGHT GILPIN TO BRIGHTON HE WAS not impressed: 'Soon after we reached Brighthelmstone, a disagreeable place. There is scarce an object either in it or near it, of nature or of art, that strikes the eye with any degree of beauty.'[8] However, when Joseph Mallord William Turner (1775–1851) visited some twenty years later he found a subject to interest him.[9] For his watercolour *Brighthelmstone* (*c.*1796) (page 10) Turner chose the historic name of the town which was by this time being supplanted by the shortened version, Brighton. The use of this archaic name was perhaps deliberate as Turner's view shows a humble coastal fishing village rather than the rapidly developing coastal resort that boasted the Prince Regent's new Pavilion. Earlier in the century Brighton's future had looked bleak as the sea encroached and the settlement dwindled, and this seems to be reflected in Turner's view, but perhaps its improving prospects are hinted at in the name of the boat drawn up on the shore in the foreground 'Hope of Brighton'. *Brighthelmstone* shares the colouring of Turner's topographic watercolours of the period, but already his interest in light, atmospheric conditions and the movement of the sea is evident.

Turner was involved in the publication of several series of prints in which views of the coast loomed large. He contributed thirty-nine watercolours, reproduced as engravings, to *Picturesque Views on the Southern Coast of*

8. Gilpin, W. (1804), *Observations on the Coasts of Hampshire, Sussex, and Kent, relative chiefly to Picturesque Beauty, made in the summer of the year 1774*, Cadell and Davies, p.42.
9. Wilton, A. (1979), *The Life and Work of J.M.W. Turner*, Academy Editions, p.315.

England, published in instalments between 1814 and 1826. He began work in the summer of 1811 and during the course of the project travelled the length of the Channel coast. Among the locations he chose to draw were Land's End, St. Michael's Mount, Plymouth, Weymouth, Lulworth Cove, Poole, Portsmouth, Brighton, Rye, Dover and Ramsgate. His love of the sea and coastline was reflected in the other print series he worked on: *Marine Views* (1822–24), *The Ports of England* (1825–28) and *Picturesque Views on the East Coast of England* (*c.*1827).

When peace was restored after 1815 artists could again move freely on the continent. Turner made two tours of Italy in 1819–20 and 1828–9, filling a succession of sketchbooks with drawings and colour studies.[10] The classical landscapes and warm light were to inform his subsequent work and not only the Italian subjects. Paintings such as *Line Fishing, off Hastings* (*c.*1835) take the forms of the south coast and elevate them to scenery fit for a classical epic. The fishermen who nonchalantly ride the swell in the foreground have a calmly heroic air and it would not be surprising to look up and see the columns of a Roman temple rising on the cliffs above. First-hand experience was very important to Turner, his memory and the wealth of material laid down in his sketchbooks were the basis of all his work, but as his career developed he was not interested in simply recreating what he saw. The American artist Edward Moran followed in his footsteps and found 'He is very inaccurate – wilfully so ... his knowledge of the forms of land and sea and cloud was so thorough that he could do pretty much as he pleased with them, and yet keep within the bounds of naturalness.'[11] Turner is undoubtedly Britain's most famous painter of sea and coast and is still probably the most celebrated artist this country has produced. Yet in his lifetime his later seascapes, today viewed as the innovative forerunners of Impressionism, were ridiculed as being unnatural and apparently unfinished. The art critic John Ruskin (1819–1900) felt compelled to devote the first volume of *Modern Painters* (1843) to a defence of Turner's approach, asserting that 'Turner *is* like nature, and paints more of nature than any man who ever lived.'[12]

AS A YOUNG MAN JOHN BRETT (1831–1902) WAS CAPTIVATED by the art of the Pre-Raphaelite Brotherhood and the writings of Ruskin. He aspired to become a figure painter in the Pre-Raphaelite style and his early work is marked by their intense colouring and the meticulous detail, drawn directly from nature, advocated by Ruskin. However, Brett's initially friendly relationship with Turner's champion soured when support gave way to pointed and rather personal criticism. Writing in 1880 of Brett's *The Val d'Aosta* (1858), Ruskin praised the 'firmness of minute execution', but felt that Brett had failed to understand the landscape in question and that he later 'took to mere photography of physical landscape and gradually lost both precision and sentiment.'[13] Ruskin's barb was perhaps tempered by the fact that in 1880 Brett was enjoying the most successful spell of his career: *Britannia's Realm* (1880) had just been bought for the Tate by the Chantrey Bequest, he had been elected an Associate of the Royal Academy and his paintings were selling well and fetching high prices. He was still producing large-scale paintings such as *Golden Prospects* (1881), a view of Land's End, in which rock, lichen, grass and the surface of the sea were rendered in minute detail. However, such paintings required painstaking work and took a great deal of time to complete, so Brett very practically made smaller, less detailed

10. Moorby, N. (2011), 'First Italian Tour 1819–20', in Blayney Brown, D. (ed.) (2012), *J.M.W. Turner: Sketchbooks, Drawings and Watercolours*: www.tate.org.uk/art/research-publications/jmw-turner/first-italian-tour-r1132344 (accessed 5 May 2015).
11. Moran, E. (1888), 'Marine Painting', in *Art Amateur*, Oct.–Nov., p.101, quoted in Riding, C. and Johns, R. (2013), *Turner and the Sea*, Thames and Hudson, p.13.
12. Ruskin, J. (1848), preface to the second edition of *Modern Painters*, vol. 1, 4th edition, Smith, Elder and Co., p.xliii.
13. Hickox, M. (2006), 'John Brett and Ruskin', in *John Brett: A Pre-Raphaelite in Cornwall*, Sansom & Co., p.41.

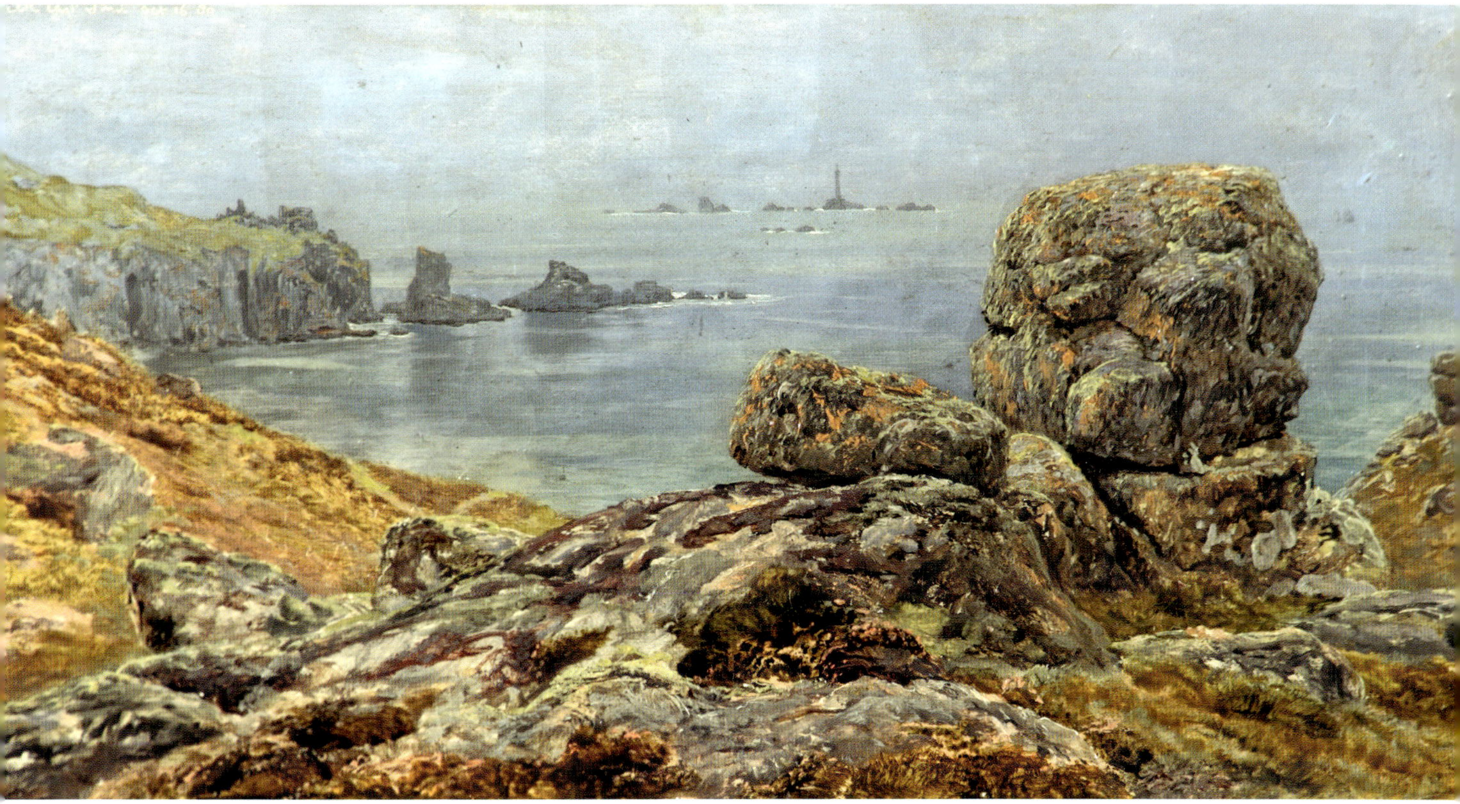

JOHN BRETT
The Land's End, Cornwall
1880 | oil on canvas | 180 x 355 mm

studies which could be produced more quickly and were also more affordable to buyers. *The Land's End, Cornwall* (1880) inscribed as *The Black East Wind*, is a variation on the view contained in *Golden Prospects* but is a fraction of the size and is painted in a much looser style. The artist looks past the foreground boulders towards Land's End and the Longships Lighthouse. The rather bleak atmosphere reflects the October weather that Brett and his family experienced during their stay at nearby Sennen: 'a strong north easterly wind which has prevailed generally since we came here some ten days ago makes the outlook dreary in the extreme, and the cold showers ... disincline one to leave the house'.[14] In such conditions Brett would make drawings and sketches on the spot and also take photographs which he used back in the studio to inform the compositions of his larger paintings.

Brett had spent his honeymoon in 1870 travelling from the Isle of Wight to explore the Dorset coast between Swanage and Lyme Regis before staying for a month on the Lizard peninsula in Cornwall. The Cornish coast obviously made a big impression and became a regular destination for the Brett family's summer expeditions. They stayed at St. Ives in 1872 where he studied the fishermen and their boats before visiting Sennen. In 1873 they toured the Scilly Isles, Penzance, St. Agnes, Tintagel and Bude. In 1876 and 1877 they returned to the Lizard. These visits continued off and on despite failing health until 1899. Brett felt that he had done much to introduce the art buying public to the attractions of Cornwall and had done so before the coastal art colonies became established in the 1880s. Over a period of thirty years he produced around two hundred views of the Cornish coast.[15]

FREDERICK GOLDEN SHORT (1863–1936) IS SOMETHING OF A rarity among the artists considered here in that he spent virtually his entire career living in his place of birth. Short was born at Lyndhurst, the son of the local chemist. His father was a keen photographer and employed the young Short to colour the magic lantern slides he used for lecturing. The budding artist went on to study at Southampton Art School and made a name for himself early on when his illustrations for F.G. Heath's book *Autumn Leaves* (1881) were reproduced in the *Illustrated London News*.[16] Although Short did go on painting tours to Devon and Cornwall during the 1880s, his abiding love was for the New Forest's glades and heaths, a subject which he was compelled to paint again and again. Strapping his paints and easel to his back he would scour the Forest, capturing the seasonal colours with a naturalistic palette. Short was certainly attracted to the coast during his tours of the west country, but he did not have to stray too far for the subject *Lymington River (View of Hurst Castle from Keyhaven)* (1901). This painting was made about ten miles from Short's home and captures the fort against the higher ground of the Isle of Wight, lit by the glow of the setting sun. It is perhaps a view that only a resident artist would find. The muddy beaches and salt marshes of Hampshire's Solent coast do not have the glamour of Kent's white cliffs or Devon's sandy bays, but to a local eye such as Short's it has a low-key beauty of its own. Sheltered by Hurst spit these marshes were once home to Lymington's salt industry and later migrating birds made them a wildfowlers' paradise. The dynamic nature of the coastal environment is also evident here. The salt marshes which expanded after the arrival of Spartina grass around 1920 are now eroding and it is thought that by 2050 they will have disappeared altogether – Short's view will be altered dramatically.

14. Brett, C. (2006), 'The Cornwall Paintings', in *John Brett: A Pre-Raphaelite in Cornwall*, Sansom & Co., p.106.
15. Brett, C. (2006), 'John Brett in Cornwall', in *John Brett: A Pre-Raphaelite in Cornwall*, Sansom & Co., p.55.
16. Marshall, S. (2002), *The Artist's New Forest, 1750–1950*, St. Barbe Museum & Art Gallery, p.36.

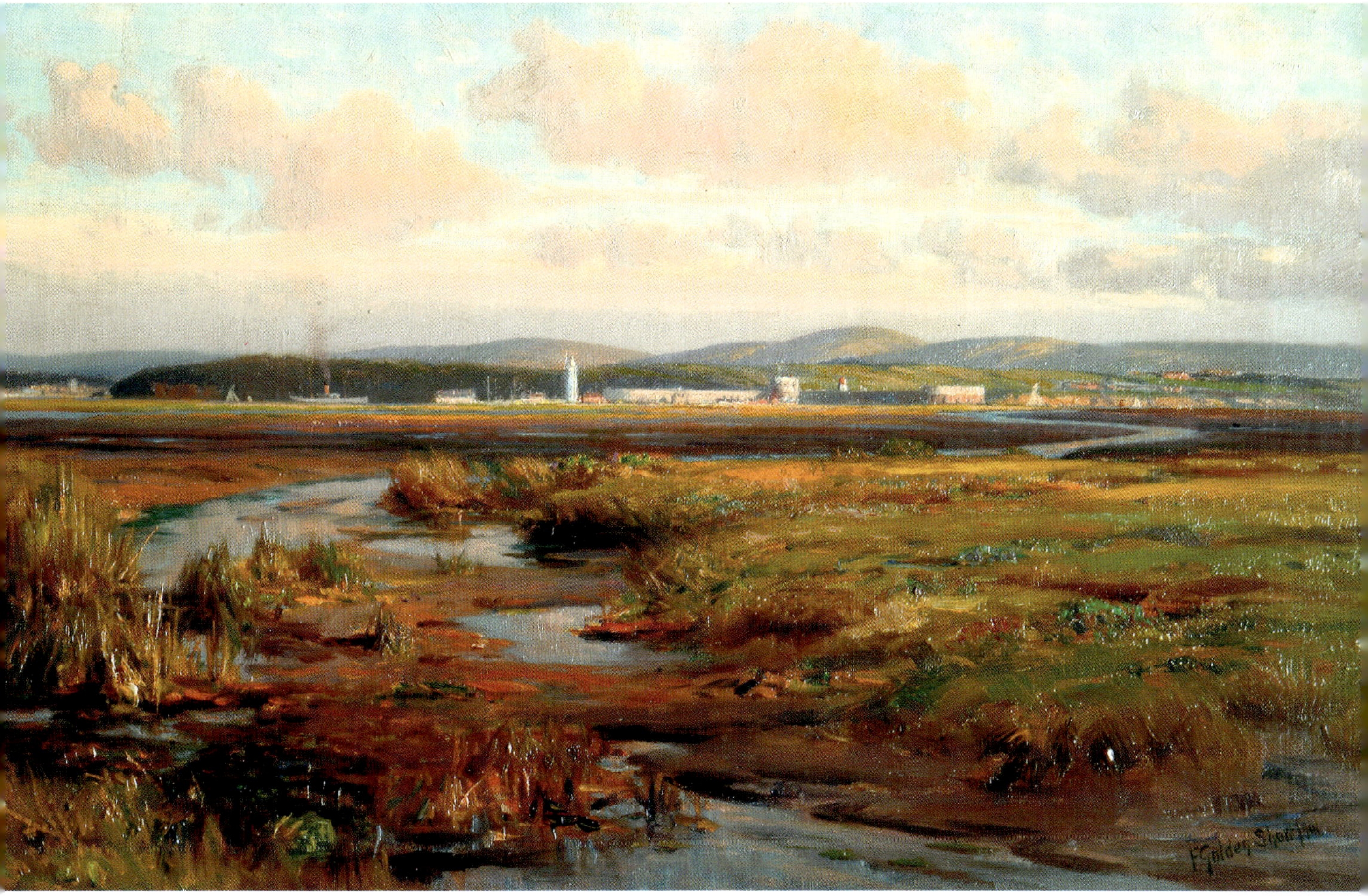

FREDERICK GOLDEN SHORT
Lymington River (View of Hurst Castle from Keyhaven)
1901 | oil on canvas | 229 x 381 mm
SOUTHAMPTON CITY ART GALLERY

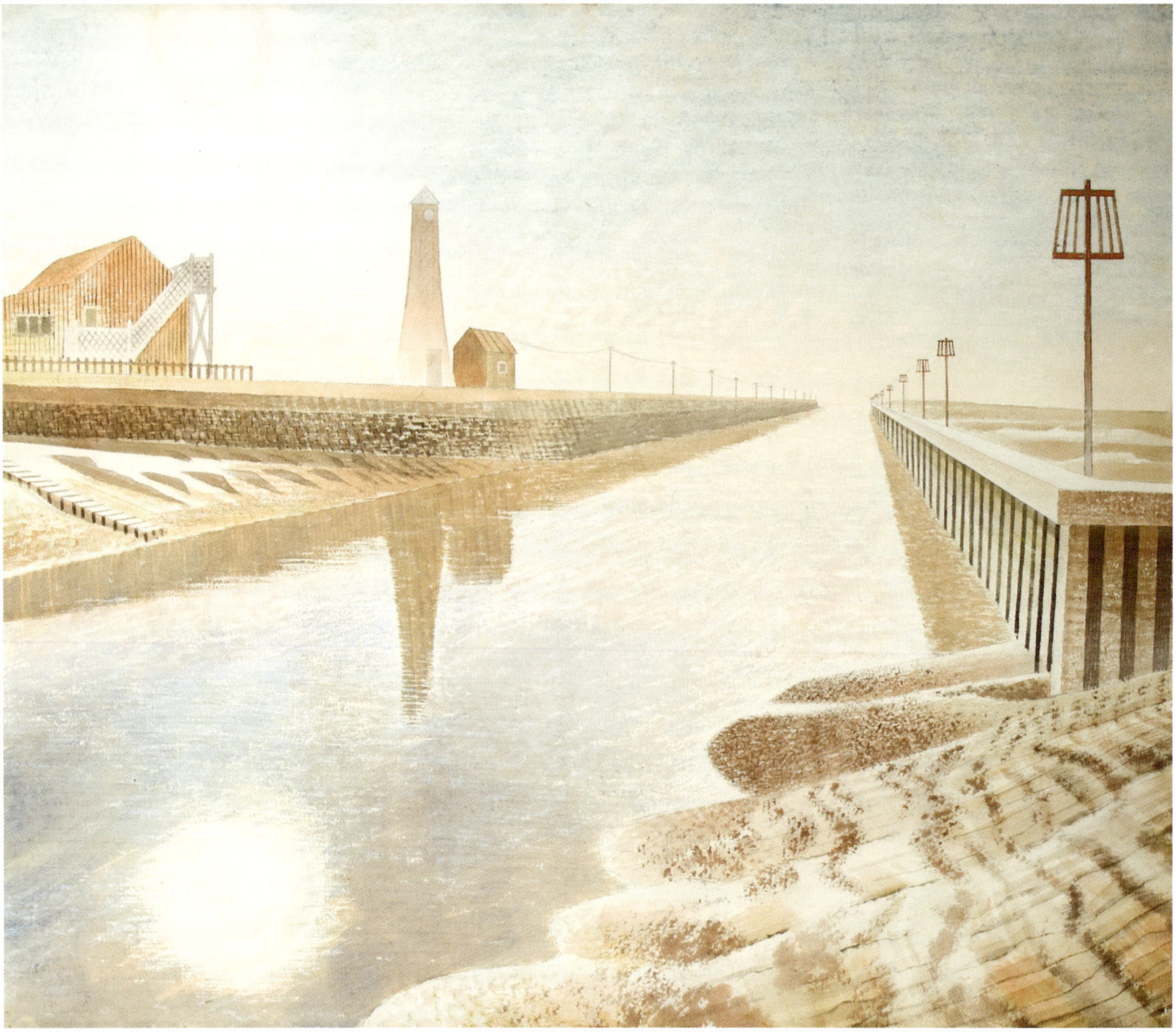

ERIC RAVILIOUS
Rye Harbour
1938 | pencil and watercolour on paper | 419 x 508 mm
IMAGE COURTESY OF THE INGRAM COLLECTION OF MODERN BRITISH & CONTEMPORARY ART

ERIC RAVILIOUS (1903–42) ROAMED RATHER MORE WIDELY THAN Short but was also regularly drawn back to the countryside and coast of his home county. Ravilious had been raised at Eastbourne in Sussex and in 1922 won a scholarship to study design at the Royal College of Art where he was taught for a time by Paul Nash. During the 1920s he worked as a wood engraver and muralist and by the 1930s had also been commissioned to design furniture and glassware as well as ceramics for Wedgwood. Despite his early death in 1942, the result of a flying accident while serving as an Official War Artist in Iceland, Ravilious's work has become increasingly popular in recent years. During his lifetime his work was always well received critically and commercially; fellow artist Vivian Pitchforth (1895–1982) once introduced him by saying 'This is Ravilious who sells all his pictures.'[17] Ravilious's watercolours are instantly recognisable and although influenced by the paintings of Francis Towne and John Sell Cotman made over a hundred years earlier, they are very much of their time. Ancient landscapes are observed with a detached objectivity and are scattered with the trappings of the modern world: barbed wire fences, trains, farm equipment, telegraph poles and even cement works.

Rye was one of the Cinque Ports, established in the 12th century to provide ships for the defence of the realm in return for tax exemptions, a degree of self-government and the right to levy tolls. These advantages made it a wealthy town, but when the harbour silted up during the 16th century its importance diminished and by the time Ravilious visited in the 1930s it was a rather genteel backwater. Ravilious had been introduced to Rye Harbour by Diana Tuely, with whom he had an affair. He wrote to her from the William the Conqueror inn where he was sleeping on a sofa until a bed became available: 'It is perfectly comfortable really, and the old beer in this pub as good as any I ever tasted.'[18] During his stay he painted the interior of the inn with a view through the window to the harbour and lighthouse. This was to be the subject of *Rye Harbour* (1938). In the same letter he explains 'I managed to work in spite of the heat, sitting in the mud with my back to a post'. While he was painting, the artist and collector Edward le Bas, who was staying nearby, came along and bought the picture on the spot. The resulting watercolour is typical of Ravilious's work in the medium. Although he did make sketches, Ravilious often started a picture on the final piece of paper, gradually developing the composition. Paintings he deemed to be failures were torn or cut up. Initial washes of colour were worked over with dry strokes in hatched or stippled patterns that perhaps owe something to the techniques of his earlier wood engravings. Ravilious enjoyed the effects of working into the light, here the base of the lighthouse begins to disappear in the glare of the sun. The painting also reflects his preference for simple compositions, in this case focused upon the neat lines of the channel, drawing the eye towards its distant vanishing point. A view that in other hands might become austere, is lightened by quirky architectural details such as the lighthouse, sheds and channel markers and the soft curves of the foreground mud. It captures the blissful calm of an already warm August morning. For Ravilious the Sussex coast had a dual attraction. On the one hand there were the functional lines of the boats, harbours and lighthouses he found at Rye and Newhaven, on the other there was the natural grandeur of the chalk cliffs at Beachy Head. He was to return to this landscape with a heightened sense of drama as a War Artist in the 1940s.

17. Binyon, H. (1983), *Eric Ravilious: Memoir of an Artist*, Lutterworth Press, p.106.
18. Ullman, A., Whittick, C. and Lawrence, S. (2008), *Eric Ravilious: Landscape, Letters and Design*, vol. 2, The Fleece Press, p.426.

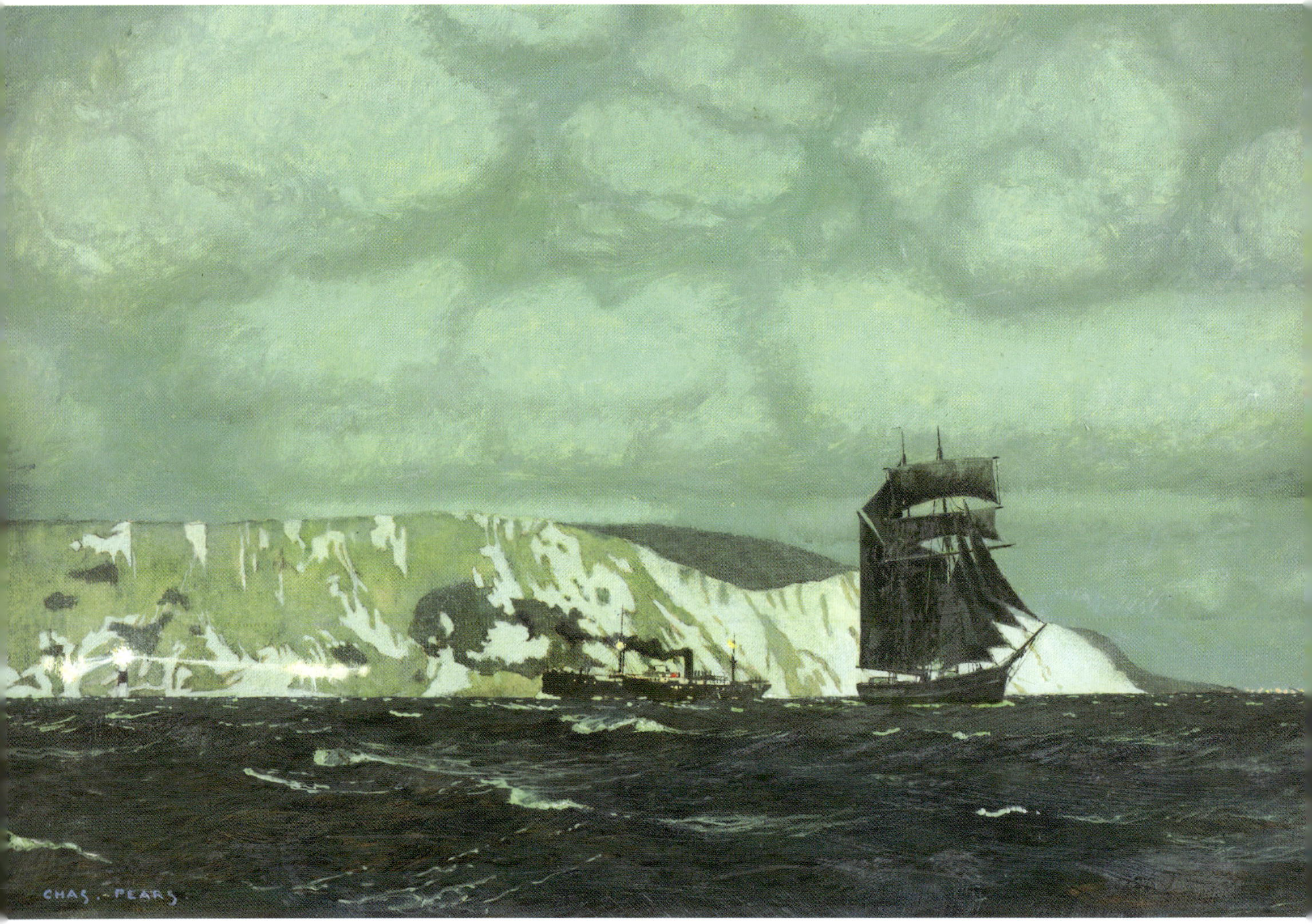

CHARLES PEARS

Beachy Head, East Sussex, Moonlight

oil on canvas | 335 x 545 mm

THE IMPOSING WALL OF CHALK AT BEACHY HEAD IS PROBABLY best seen from the sea and this was the view that Charles Pears (1873–1958) chose for his atmospheric oil painting *Beachy Head, East Sussex, Moonlight* (undated). He shows a brigantine, silhouetted against the cliffs, sailing out across the Channel while a brightly lit steamer passes behind. The lights of Bexhill and Hastings are just visible on the far right. The Beachy Head Lighthouse was built at the base of the cliffs in 1902, replacing the Belle Toute Lighthouse on the headland above. Here it sends out its beams, warning ships away from the cliffs, which Pears shows patched with green vegetation. The Channel's chalk cliffs are kept white by a process of erosion: the sea undercuts from the bottom, while in winter water in the rock swells as it freezes cracking away sections of chalk above. Chunks of the cliffs then collapse into the water exposing fresh white chalk. The rubble at the base of the cliffs protects them for a while, allowing plants to get a hold on the surface until the whole process begins again. At Beachy Head the cliffs are disappearing at a rate of up to a meter each year, the Belle Toute Lighthouse had to be moved back in 1999 to prevent it from falling into the sea.

Pears is one of the most celebrated marine painters of the twentieth century and was the first elected President of the Royal Society of Marine Artists which was founded in 1939. He also served as an Official War Artist in both World Wars. However, Pears is best known as a prolific poster artist who worked for railway companies, London Underground and the Empire Marketing Board. His work for Southern Railway took him to a number of locations on the south coast including Ramsgate (1926), Hastings (1947), Brighton and Hove (1935), Southsea (1936), Southampton (1930) and the Isle of Wight (1935) and he also made a poster promoting Paignton (1938) for the Great Western Railway. He captured these places with the warm colours and bright graphic style required of the medium in what was a golden age for British poster art. During the nineteenth century the expanding railway network had enabled city-dwellers to visit places on the coast which had formerly been inaccessible except by long and uncomfortable journeys in horse-drawn coaches. By the beginning of the twentieth century people were pouring out of the cities and heading to the coast in ever-increasing numbers, many no doubt encouraged by the idyllic scenes presented on the railway companies' advertising posters.

BY THE 1930S THE PROLIFERATION OF THE MOTOR CAR MEANT that even parts of the coast too remote to be reached by rail were coming within the reach of travellers. Taking a leaf out of the railway companies' book, Shell commissioned some of the leading artists of the day to create posters encouraging drivers to explore the riches of the British landscape in cars powered by Shell petrol. Paul Nash (1889–1946) designed several posters for the company including *Kimmeridge Folly, Dorset* (1937), part of the *To Visit Britain's Landmarks* series. It takes a view from the beach looking up towards Clavell Tower, a folly built on the headland in 1830. The poster has the heightened atmosphere of the surreal work Nash created during time spent at Swanage between 1933 and 1936. The wall at the bottom of the cliffs is greatly exaggerated, searchlight beams from the sun point to the tower and the sea and there is a uncanny intensity to the rocks and seaweed lying on the shoreline. In Nash's time the tower was semi-derelict and in recent years its future was called into question by the erosion of the shale cliffs. In the end

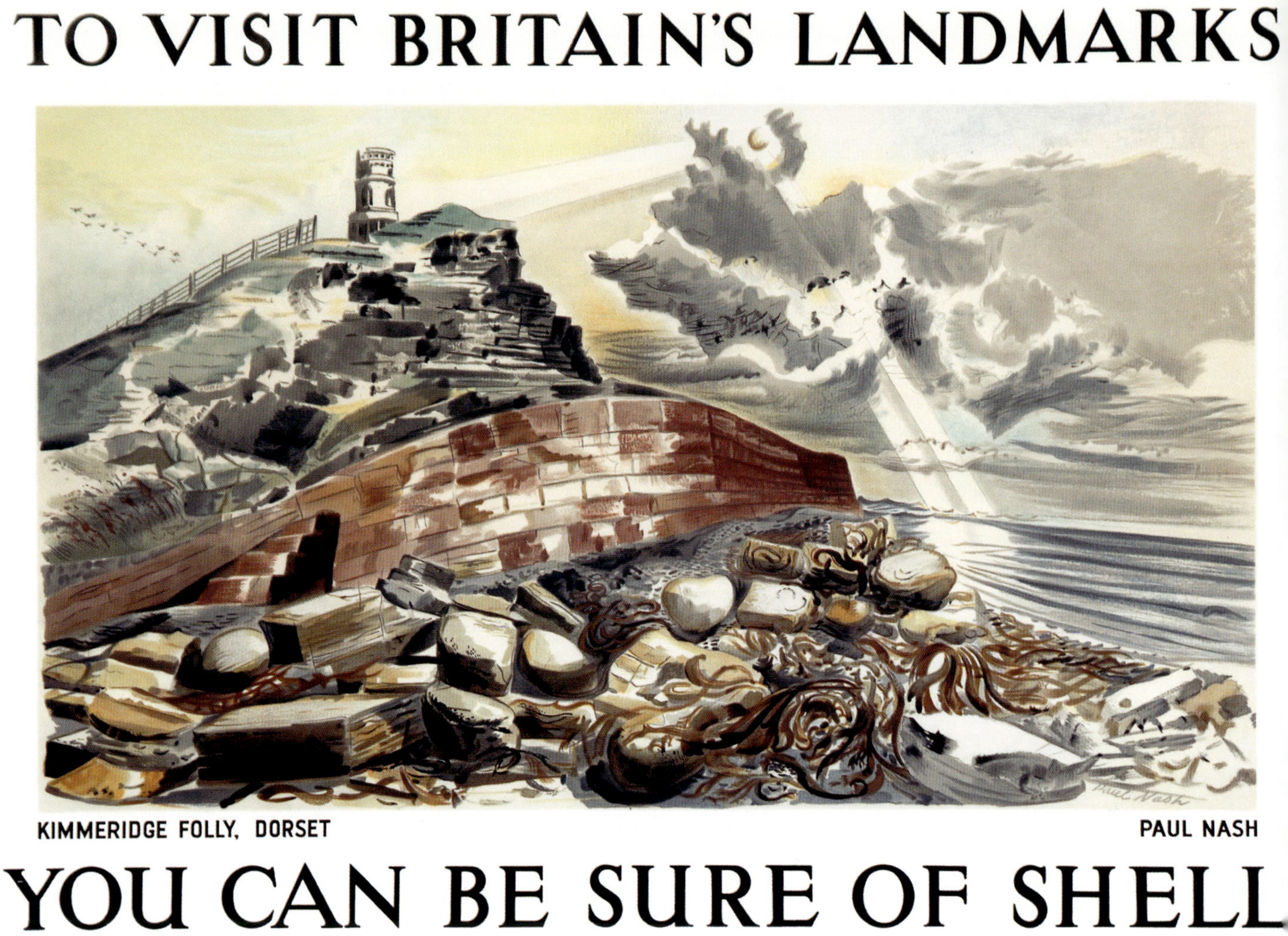

PAUL NASH
Kimmeridge Folly, Dorset
1937 | poster | 545 x 780 mm
COURTESY THE SHELL ART COLLECTION, SHELL BRANDS INTERNATIONAL AG

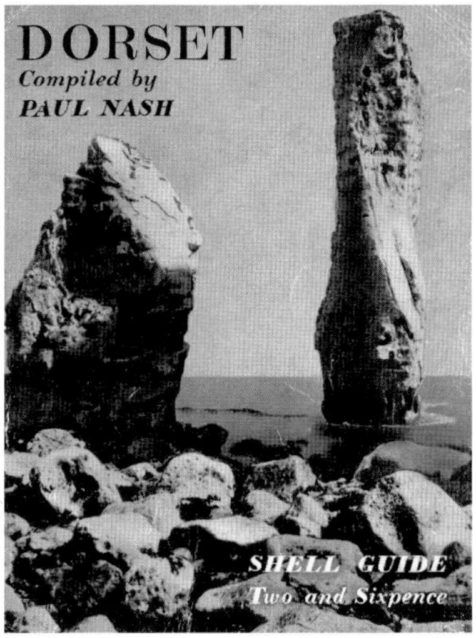

PAUL NASH
Shell Guide to Dorset
1936 | book
COURTESY THE SHELL ART COLLECTION, SHELL BRANDS INTERNATIONAL AG

it was dismantled and laboriously reconstructed twenty-five metres further back, before re-opening as a holiday cottage in 2008.

When Nash came to the Dorset coast in the 1930s he was renewing an acquaintance first made on childhood holidays. In his autobiography he recalled the impression it made on his younger self:

> I had come far afield. Beyond the boundary hedges the downs, threaded with juniper and other scrub, mounted to the spine of the great headland that arched up against the blue sky. From the summit a precipitous chalk cliff fell sheer to the sea. The still afternoon was disturbed only by the thin cries of the gulls. I was in Dorset, where we now came every year for our summer holidays. The cliff before me was Ballard Head rising up in majesty over Swanage Bay ... I remembered the curious sense of being alone in the wide fields, the spacious scene beyond emphasising a sense of the power I felt in this isolation.[19]

The pleasure Nash took in isolation and the importance he laid on 'genius loci', the mysterious spirit of place, was rather at odds with his work for Shell, which effectively encouraged the masses to set off in their cars to explore (and perhaps spoil) these magical places. He rapidly became disillusioned with Swanage: 'Every day it seemed more unbearably vulgar. The people who live there, my God, the people who come there on the buses and steamers – beyond belief.'[20] It is telling that when he was commissioned by John Betjeman (1906–84) to compile the *Shell Guide to Dorset* (1936) he dedicated it to 'The landowners of Dorset, the Council for the Preservation of Rural England, the Society for the Protection of Ancient Buildings and all those courageous enemies of "development" to whom we owe what is left of England.'[21] The guide is very much a reflection of Nash's interests and obsessions, dwelling on the geological bones of the county, its history, ancient landscapes and monuments rather than the county's towns or architecture. Of its shoreline he said 'The sea coast of Dorset, considering its comparatively short extent, must be one of the most varied and exciting in England. Geologically, it is of unique interest, showing in a lively and dramatic way the effect of the sea's influence on its different compositions.'[22]

THIS IS CERTAINLY A VIEW THAT WOULD BE SHARED BY JEREMY Gardiner (b. 1957) who, like Nash, was introduced to the area during childhood holidays – his grandmother lived at Swanage. Gardiner's early years were marked by regular uprooting as the family followed in the wake of his father's army postings. They eventually settled in Bushey in Hertfordshire but by then the Dorset coast was established as a critical part of his world: 'Dorset is the baseline for all my work, the one place I go back to ... It's important to leave and then return in order to understand a place properly – you've got the contrast and context then'.[23] That fresh perspective was provided, after the completion of his artistic training, by an extended period living and working in the United States between 1984 and 1998. It was during this sojourn that he came upon an article 'Swanage or Seaside Surrealism' written by Paul Nash in the *Architectural Review*. This inspired Gardiner to rent the seafront property in which Nash had stayed while he was writing the Shell guide in 1935. The result was the *Ballard Point* (1998) series of paintings which investigated the changing appearance of the headland through the seasons and under the ephemeral effects of light and weather conditions.

19. Nash, P. (1949), *Outline: An Autobiography*, Faber and Faber, p.121.
20. Nash, P. (1935), letter to Ruth Clark, c. July 1935, quoted in Denton, P. (2002), *Seaside Surrealism: Paul Nash in Swanage*, Peveril Press, p.51.
21. Nash, P. (1936), *Shell Guide to Dorset*, Architectural Press, p.6.
22. Ibid., p.15.
23. Collins, I. (2013), 'In the Beginning: Deep Mining in Dorset', in *The Art of Jeremy Gardiner: Unfolding Landscape*, Lund Humphries, p.10.

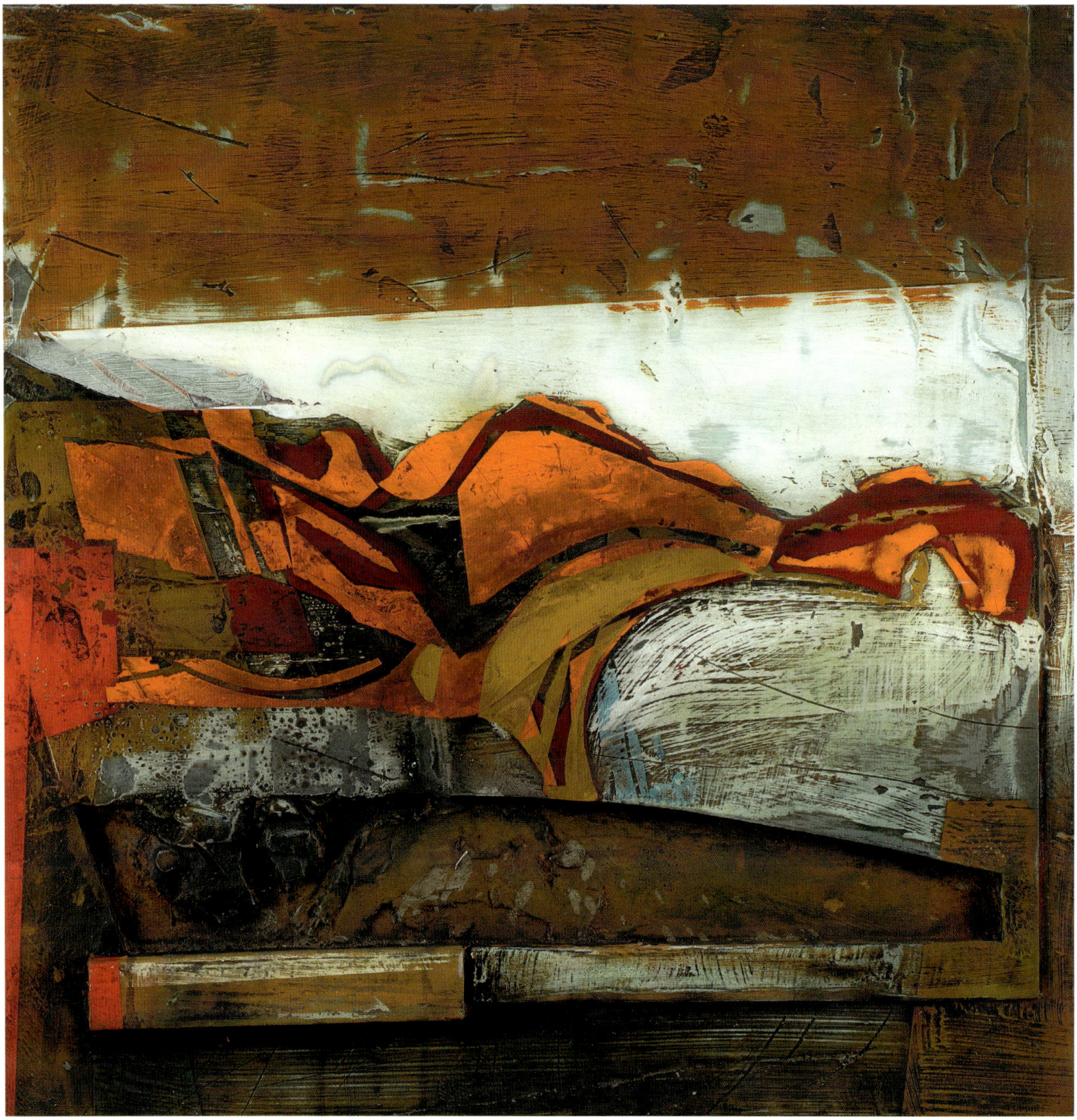

JEREMY GARDINER
Durdle Door, Sunrise
2007 | acrylic and jesmonite on panel | 600 x 600 mm

Observing the view from inside the room also resulted in the inclusion of Ben Nicholson-inspired cubist still life assemblages. 'I worked indoors, looking from relative darkness at the brilliant light on Swanage Bay, from an enclosed place to a vast expanse of sea and sky ... The horizontal plane of the bay and the oblique shafts of light create a unique spectacle, but the weather changes and the scene is gone as quickly as it has arrived.'[24] Gardiner also painted the folly at Kimmeridge, but in *Clavell Tower, Kimmeridge* (2009) it appears as a tiny detail for which the viewer has to hunt, almost lost in the geological enormity of the Dorset coast.

This section of the Channel shoreline is now part of the Jurassic Coast, a World Heritage Site which runs from Orcombe Point in Devon to Old Harry Rocks near Swanage. Its rocks and fossils provide an unparalleled record spanning 185 million years of pre-history through the Triassic, Jurassic and Cretaceous periods. The stretch between Lyme Regis and Ballard Point is a constant source of inspiration for Gardiner who is acutely aware of the almost unimaginable scale of geological time in which human history represents the most fleeting of moments. The battering of the sea has sculpted the differing rock formations into some of the most startling features on the British coast, perhaps the most iconic of these being Durdle Door. This limestone arch has been the subject of several Gardiner paintings including *Durdle Door, Sunrise* (2007):

> The name Durdle is derived from the Old English word 'thirl' meaning drill or bore and the 'Door' or natural arch, has been cut and sculpted by the waves in vertical Portland Stone. When painting this remarkable subject, I have tried to give it a presence and personality that sets it apart from the rest of the Jurassic Coastline. The layers of paint, scraped down and over-painted create intermingled strata, echoing the multiplicity of memories that inform the work. 'Sunrise, Durdle Door' is about spirit and sense of place, evoking a keen understanding of a particular landscape; its contours and unique history.[25]

The support for many of his paintings has been plywood, shaped with routers and gouges to create a three-dimensional relief. This surface can then be excavated, much as the sea bites into rock, or built up using jesmonite, a material employed by palaeontologists to make casts of fossils. Gardiner uses water-based acrylics which dry rapidly and can be quickly over-painted to create layers of colour. These in turn can be scraped away to reveal the strata of paint below, a technique which mirrors the processes of weathering and erosion. In this way the finished painting may contain elements of several different pictures.[26]

TO GAIN A DEEPER UNDERSTANDING OF THE LANDSCAPE

Gardiner has explored the coast 'not only on foot but also on a bicycle, from out at sea in a boat and from above in a light aircraft – in order to see familiar places from unfamiliar perspectives.'[27] His interest in accommodating these different viewpoints, sometimes within the same painting, continues a practice that was central to the work of Peter Lanyon (1918–64). For Lanyon this experience had to be reflected not only in the finished work but also in the physical actions involved in making it: 'I merely state my preference for painting as being a recreation of experience in immediacy, a process of being, made now.'[28] Underlying this desire to capture the moment

24. Gardiner, J. (2010), artist's commentary on *Summer Storm and Sunlight, Old Harry* (2009), in *Jeremy Gardiner: A Panoramic View*, Paisnel Gallery.
25. Gardiner, J. (2015), personal correspondence with the author, May 2015.
26. Martin, S. (2013), 'The Process of Finding Out: On Jeremy Gardiner's Working Methods', in *The Art of Jeremy Gardiner: Unfolding Landscape*, Lund Humphries, p.124.
27. Gardiner, J. (2010), artist's commentary on *Spring, Durdle Door* (2009), in *Jeremy Gardiner: A Panoramic View*, Paisnel Gallery.
28. Lanyon, P. (1959), 'Landscape: Coast Journey and Painting', recorded talk quoted in Lewis, D. (1996), 'St. Ives: A Personal Memoir, 1947–55', in *St. Ives 1939–64: Twenty Five Years of Painting, Sculpture and Pottery*, Tate Gallery Publishing, revised edition, p.39.

was a keen appreciation of the cultural and historical significance of the landscape. Lanyon was born in St. Ives and was descended from long-established Cornish families which had been involved in the tin mining industry. As a young man he studied with Borlase Smart (1881–1947), painting landscapes out of doors, but the arrival of Ben Nicholson and Naum Gabo in St. Ives at the start of the Second World War encouraged Lanyon towards constructivism and abstraction. When he returned to the area in 1946 after wartime service with the Royal Air Force it was with a renewed sense of belonging, but Cornwall was changing, traditional industries were dying out and a new economy based on tourism was evolving. Lanyon's post-war work embodies these complex and apparently opposing influences, as Andrew Causey puts it: 'The confrontation in his art between modernism of technique and the elegiac character of some of his themes is distinctive, and warns against assuming a necessary connection between modernism and modernity.'[29]

Lanyon's approach is typified by *Porthleven* (1950–1) which was bought for the Tate and did much to establish his reputation. Lanyon made many sketches of the coastal fishing port and these different viewpoints are incorporated as overlapping components of the wider composition, one of the few obviously recognisable landmarks being the clock tower at the very top of the painting. Lanyon also suggested that 'water runs right down the middle of the picture, which is rather like an aerial view' and that the forms on the left and right of the painting could be read as figures: 'This may be accidental, or at any rate unconscious, but I always look for figures in my paintings when I have painted them.'[30] These he felt could be identified as a fisherman with a lamp facing his wife wrapped in a shawl, symbolic of the town's social and cultural heritage. Paintings of coastal communities such as Porthleven also reflect Lanyon's love of the Cornish shore: 'I like to paint places where solids and fluids come together, such as the meeting of sea and cliff, of wind and rock, of human body and water.'[31] The tones of Cornwall's grassy headlands and the surrounding sea had informed Lanyon's palette of greens and blues, but exposure to the warmth and colour of the United States and Mexico in 1963–4 saw bolder 'unnatural' colours appear in his compositions. While not as overtly bright as works like *Glide Path* (1964), the gouache painting *Dark Mine Coast* (1964) reflects this progression. This is one of the last works he completed before his untimely death as the result of a gliding accident – he had taken to the skies in search of an aerial perspective on the landscape. Although in comparison to much British landscape painting Lanyon's work can at first sight seem wholly abstract, he saw himself as part of a tradition stretching back to Turner and Constable. But rather than repeating what had come before he was intent on re-imagining the subject, trying to convey not just the physical components of a location but his subjective experience of it as a place defined as much by its cultural history as its outward appearance.

29. Causey, A. (2006), *Peter Lanyon: Modernism and the Land*, Reaktion Books, pp.7–8.
30. Ibid., pp.86–7.
31. Lanyon, P. (1963), transcript of British Council lecture quoted in Stephens, C. (2000), *Peter Lanyon: At the Edge of Landscape*, 21 Publishing, p.19.

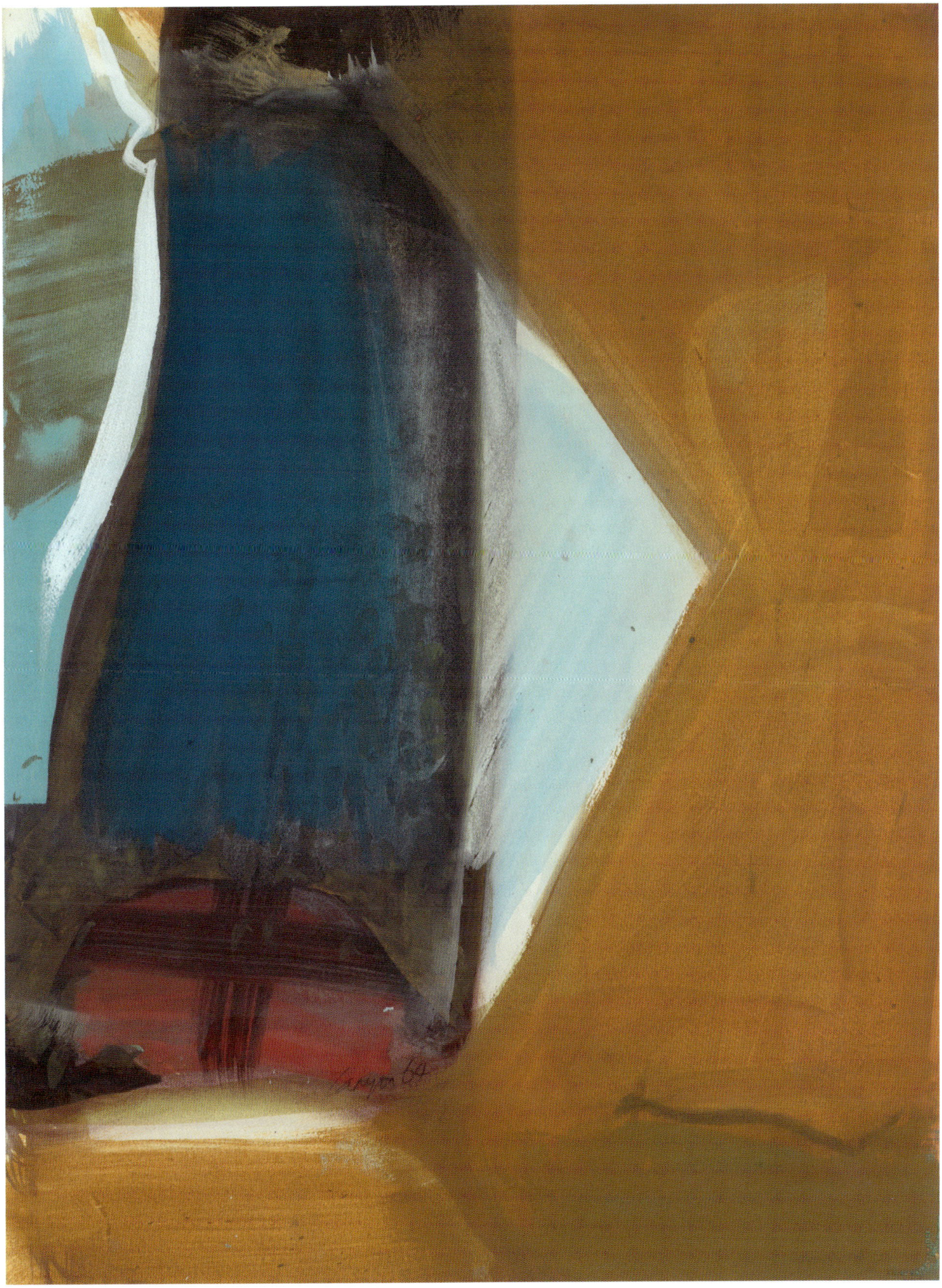

PETER LANYON
Dark Mine Coast
1964 | gouache on paper | 764 x 578 mm

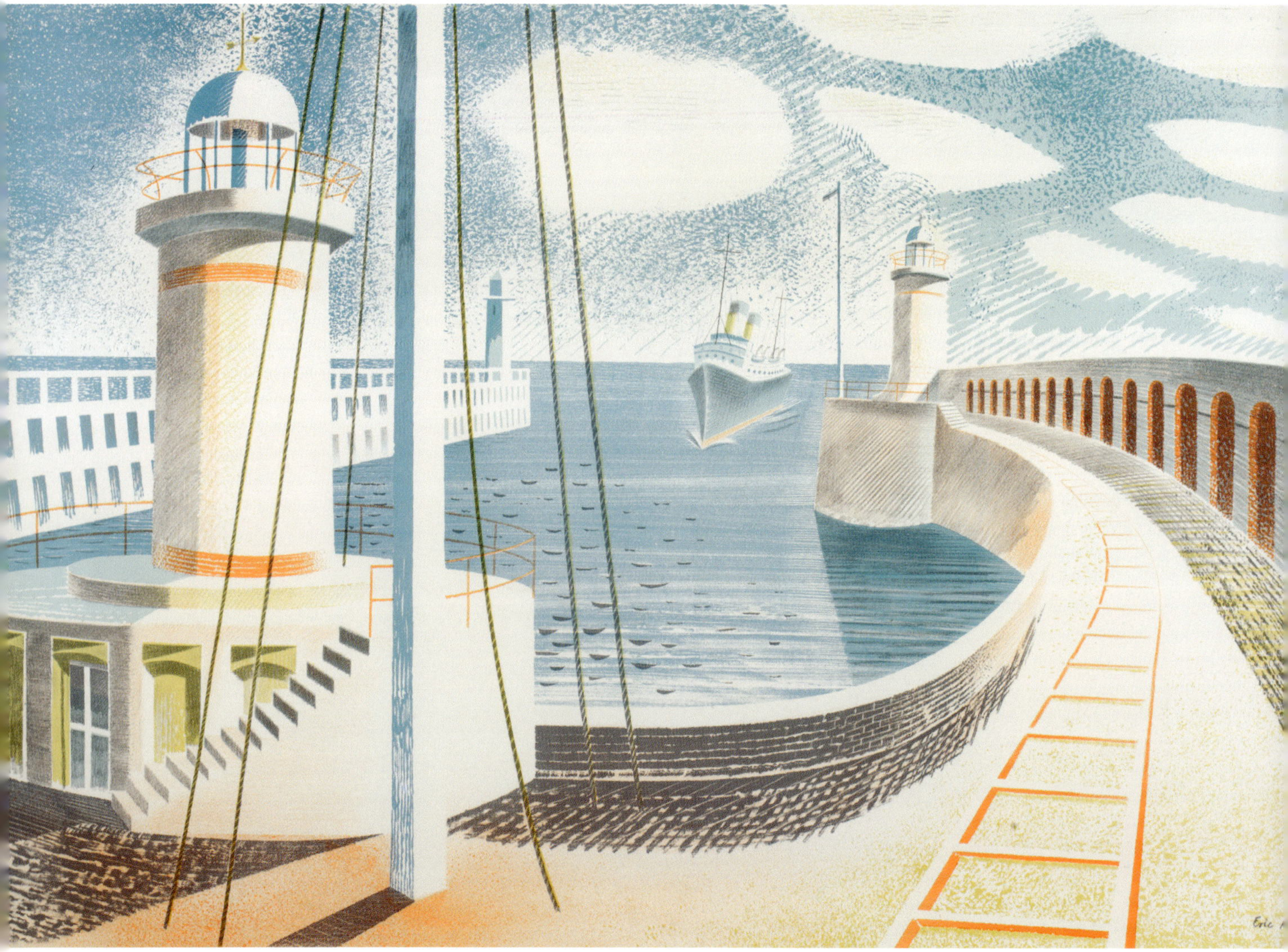

ERIC RAVILIOUS
Newhaven Harbour
1937 | lithograph on paper | 335 x 545 mm
VICTORIA AND ALBERT MUSEUM

STORMS AND SAFE HAVENS

STEVE MARSHALL

FOR AN ISLAND NATION LIKE BRITAIN THE SEA WAS FOR centuries the only means to communicate and trade with the wider world. Those with the initiative and bravery to venture out on the waves gained access to new markets, goods, cultures, ideas and a year-round harvest. However, in order to reap these rewards Britain's merchants, sailors and fishermen often placed their lives at the mercy of the elements. The inhabitants of Britain's coasts were acutely aware of the desperate plight of those caught in a storm at sea. At such times the shore could represent safety in the form of a port, harbour or convenient beach, but it might equally spell disaster: wooden ships driven onto rocks could disintegrate in a matter of minutes. Inland, storms could just as easily damage property or bring down trees, but on the coast the force of the wind took visible form in the fearful raging of the sea.

The drama of the storm, both natural and human, provided compelling subject matter for British artists from the eighteenth century onwards. At first, the influence of Dutch marine art was reflected in paintings of storms and wrecks which could be interpreted as an allegory for the trials and tribulations encountered on man's journey through life. However, there was also a growing demand for representations of famous wrecks and the public's appetite for the horrors of actual events was also reflected in the popularity of narratives recording every detail of a ship's destruction and the resulting loss of life. It might seem odd for a seafaring nation to decorate their walls with paintings of ships foundering at sea, but at the same time as Britain was establishing herself as the world's foremost maritime power writers including the philosopher Edmund Burke (1729–97) were developing the aesthetics of the sublime. In *A Philosophical Enquiry into the Origin of our Ideas of the Sublime and Beautiful* (1757), Burke expressed the idea that in addition to the pleasure we take in beauty, there is also a delight to be gained from feelings of terror. The vicarious thrill of witnessing a shipwreck on canvas was in part due to the knowledge that the sight was not real and the viewer in no danger. The acceptance of such ideas meant that awe-inspiring landscapes such as mountains or cliffs and the violence of storms at sea became more widely accepted as suitable subjects for paintings. When Turner painted *The Shipwreck* in 1805 he was continuing a tradition brought to Britain by the Van de Veldes and subsequently developed by the likes of Peter Monamy (1681–1749), Charles Brooking and Philip James de Loutherbourg (1740–1812).

However, by the Victorian period there was an increasing reluctance to contemplate the horrific reality of wrecks.[1] The inclusion of attempts at rescue from boats or from the shore added an element of hope to such pictures, making them more palatable to picture buyers. New safety measures such as the lighthouses which gradually spread along the Channel coast also proved a popular subject: the Eddystone Lighthouse, first built in 1698, was painted by Monamy, Clarkson Stanfield (1793–1867) and Richard Brydges Beechey (1808–95) among others.

The English Channel is a busy waterway, not only connecting Britain with the continent, but also providing the safest route for vessels heading to and from the North Sea and the Baltic. Such a volume of shipping has inevitably made the south coast a prime wreck site, with the shores of Kent and Cornwall being particularly dangerous. The Goodwin Sands, known as the 'Great Swallower of Ships', lie four miles off the Kent coast between Dover and Ramsgate. Over the centuries it is thought that thousands of ships have run aground and disappeared into these shifting sands. At low tide the sandbars are, in places, firm enough for a walk, a picnic or even a cricket match, but as the waters rise they can turn into a deadly quicksand capable of sucking down an entire ship. The sands also have a habit of regurgitating old wrecks for a time, only to swallow them once more. The stretch of water between the sands and the coast known as 'the Downs' offers some shelter from the waves and currents of the Channel, but in severe weather that shelter has proved illusory. The Great Storm of December 1703 saw thirteen British warships lost along with over two thousand sailors. In his essay *The Storm*, Daniel Defoe described the area as:

> The Fatal Goodwin, where the wreck of Navies lies
> A thousand dying sailors talking to the skies[2]

A number of artists have painted wrecks and rescues around the Goodwin Sands. Perhaps the most striking treatment is by William Lionel Wyllie (1851–1931). Wyllie was born in London and studied at the Royal Academy Schools. He settled in Portsmouth in 1871. Today he is viewed as one of Britain's greatest marine painters whose fascination with all aspects of maritime life provides an absorbing record of military, commercial and leisure vessels around the coasts and rivers of England. *The Goodwin Sands, Kent* (1874) embodies the 'pre-occupation with keenly observed atmospheric and meteorological effect' prevalent in his early work.[3] Although Wyllie often made oil sketches directly from nature and as a keen sailor he may well have witnessed this scene first-hand, this is a painting very much concerned with the poetry of the subject. The artist emphasised this in his choice of a passage from Shakespeare as the subtitle for the work:

> the Goodwins, I think they call the place; a very
> dangerous flat and fatal, where the carcasses of many
> a tall ship lie buried[4]

The foreground is dominated by the protruding ribs of a wrecked boat. Beyond, another damaged ship has run aground and is being attended by a number of smaller boats. Whether these are engaged in rescuing crew and salvaging cargo or illicitly helping themselves to the goods on board is open to question: the Deal boatmen who were praised for rescuing sailors from the

1. Payne, C. (2007), *Where the Sea Meets the Land: Artists on the Coast in Nineteenth Century Britain*, Sansom & Co., p.141.
2. Defoe, D. (1704), *The Storm: An Essay*, lines 120–121.
3. Quarm, R. (1981), 'On the Shore: 1860–1880', in *W. L. Wyllie Marine Artist, 1851–1931*, Chris Beetles, p.50.
4. Shakespeare, W., *The Merchant of Venice*, Act 3, Scene 1.

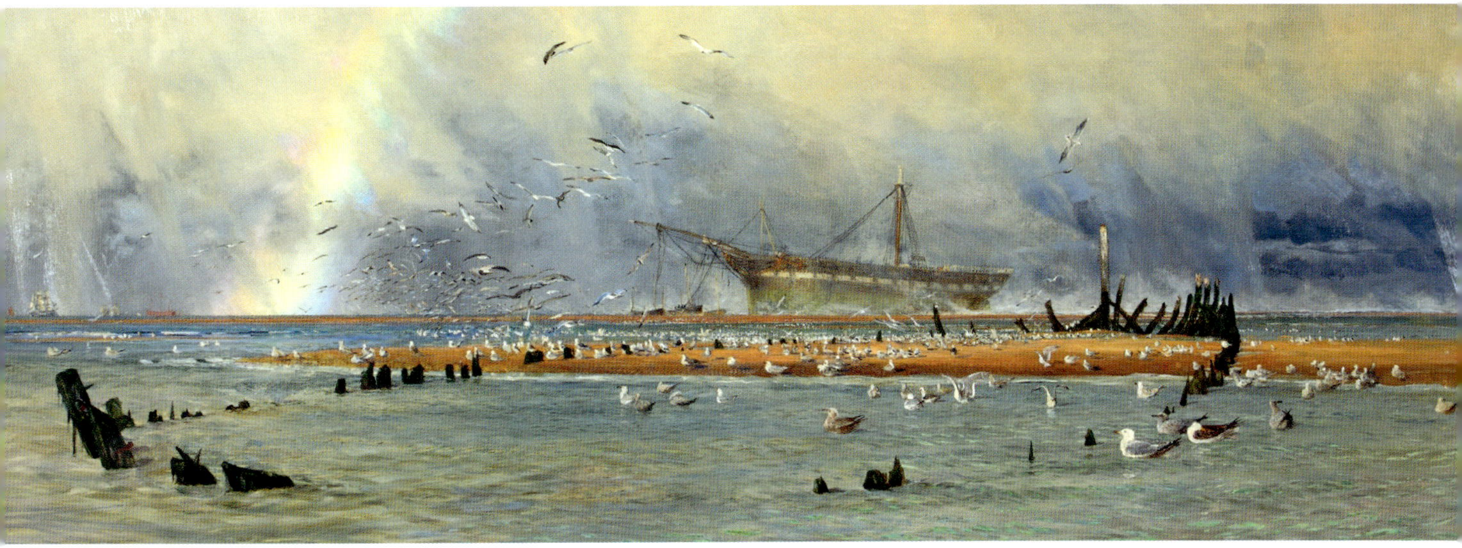

WILLIAM LIONEL WYLLIE
The Goodwin Sands, Kent
1874 | oil on canvas | 593 x 1800 mm

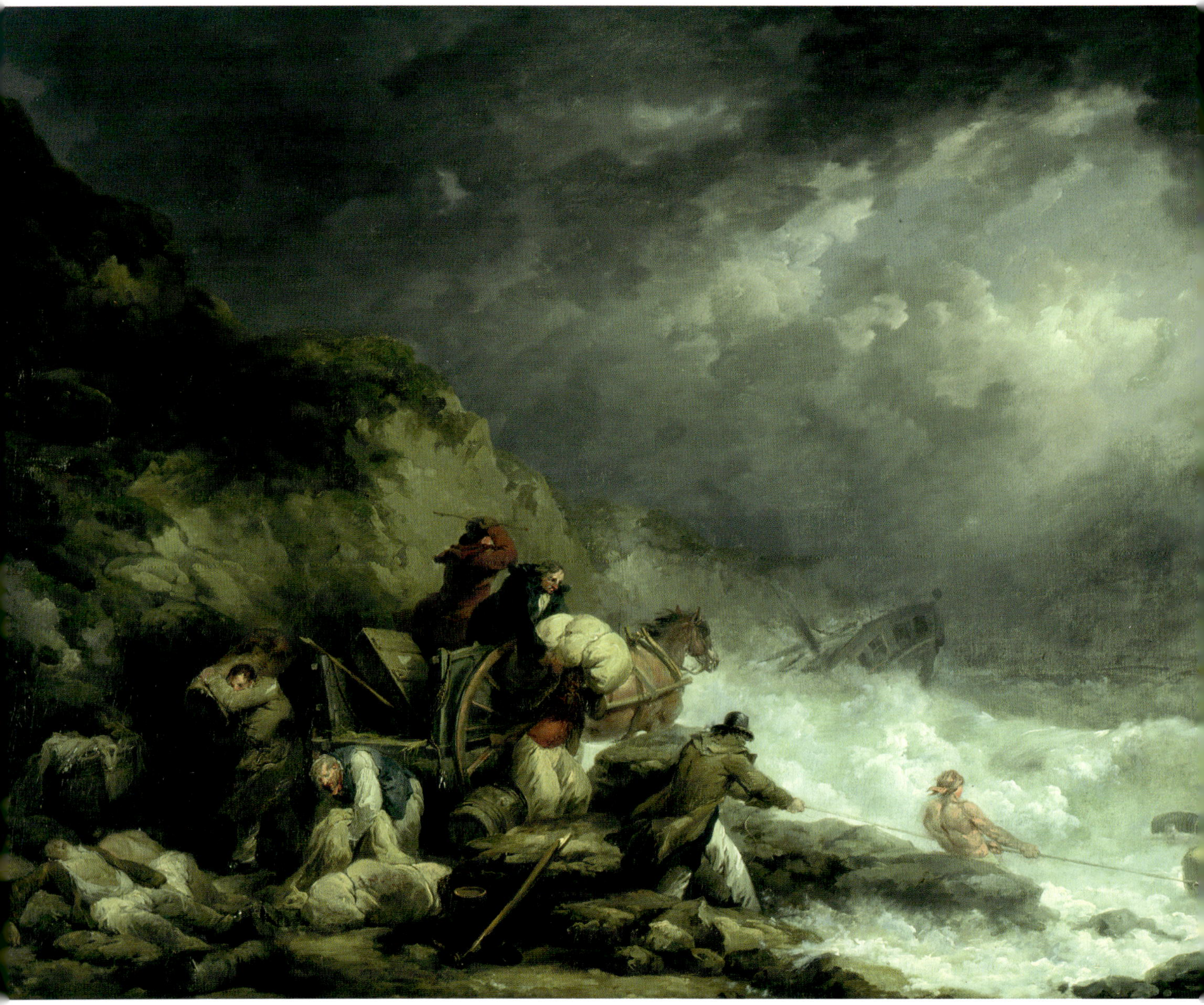

GEORGE MORLAND
The Wreckers
*c.*1791 | oil on canvas | 1028 x 1385 mm
SOUTHAMPTON CITY ART GALLERY

sands were also implicated in the plundering of wrecks on several occasions during the nineteenth century.[5] The rainbow may herald the saving of this ship, or perhaps its fate is indicated by the skeletal timbers emerging from the sands. Just visible to the left of the rainbow is a red-painted lightvessel. Wyllie's canvas was created in the year a fourth lightvessel, the *East Goodwin*, was introduced as part of ongoing attempts to save shipping from the sands. The lightships themselves were not immune to the dangers and as recently as 1954 the sands tragically claimed the *South Goodwin* lightvessel and all seven of its crew. The area remains a hazard today, marked out by a series of lighted buoys and the unmanned *East Goodwin* lightvessel.

AFTER KENT, CORNWALL BOASTS THE MOST WRECKS OF ANY British county, but here the subject has become bound up with the idea of brutal wreckers luring ships on to the shore and murdering passengers and crew in order to seize the cargo. This idea has become fixed in the popular imagination, partly in response to contemporary accounts, such as that written by Daniel Defoe in the 1720s, in which he states 'this part of Cornwall may truly be said to be inhabited by a fierce and ravenous people; for they are so greedy, and eager for the prey, that they are charg'd with strange, bloody, and cruel dealings' and where the unfortunate sailors 'find the rocks themselves not more merciless than the people who range about them for their prey.'[6] Certainly wrecking was a significant problem and the law was stiffened as a result. In 1714 entering a vessel without permission, obstructing the saving of a ship or goods, or carrying off goods without permission would result in a year in prison, while deliberate wrecking by making holes or stealing a ship's pump carried the death penalty. In 1753 death became the punishment for anyone caught plundering, taking away goods, attacking survivors or deliberately wrecking by putting out false lights.[7] However, little evidence has been found for wrecks being caused by the showing of lights and it is difficult to prove that murder was committed although there is no doubt that robbery was common.[8] In fact in the majority of cases the local population was actively involved in attempting to save lives. When Commodore Walker's ship *Boscawen* was grounded in 1745 he praised the people of St. Ives who 'flocked down in numbers to our assistance; and, at the risk of many of their own lives, saved ours'.[9] Admittedly elements of he local populace did then plunder the contents of the ship. In most cases wrecking simply meant the harvesting of flotsam and jetsam washed up on the shore. People would help themselves to food or drink that might supplement a meagre diet, or goods that could be sold to alleviate the poverty in which many lived. For those dwelling by the coast a wreck was seen literally as a godsend, an act of providence which gave them a natural right to goods offered up by the sea. The government and the owners of ships and cargoes saw things rather differently.

Of course the idea of the murderous wrecker provides a far more dramatic subject for painting or prose. *The Wreckers* (*c.*1791) by George Morland (1763–1804) is ambiguous on this point. He shows a group of men, suddenly illuminated by a break in the clouds, busy claiming the contents of a ship which has been smashed on the rocks beyond. Some load a cart with their booty, while others struggle to haul in a bale and are perhaps in danger of being dashed upon the rocks themselves. Trying to seize goods at the height of a storm was hazardous and wreckers might easily be sucked out by the

5. Bower, J., *The Deal Boatmen: Heroes or Villains*, p.9, Kent Archaeological Society On-line Publishing, Series One: www.kentarchaeology.ac/authors/authors.html (accessed 24 April 2015).
6. Defoe, D. (1724), *A Tour Through the Whole Island of Great Britain*, vol. 1, Dent Everyman's Library, 1962, pp.243–44.
7. Pearce, C.J. (2010), *Cornish Wrecking 1700–1860: Reality and Popular Myth*, Boydell Press, p.63 and 68.
8. Ibid., p.69.
9. Walker, G. (1760), *Voyages and Cruises of Commodore Walker*, vol. 1, A. Millar, p.232.

waves to meet the same fate as the broken ship and its crew. On the far left of the canvas are two corpses and the viewer must decide whether these men were already drowned and washed ashore, or met their fate at the hands of wreckers wanting to protect their identity or ensure a 'dead wreck' from which no survivor might claim the cargo. Morland painted more than one version of *The Wreckers* and another painting on the subject *The Cornish Plunderers*, showing people going through chests and trunks washed up from a wreck, was considered by his biographer to be his finest work.[10] George Morland's life reads likes a 'Rake's Progress' of which William Hogarth or Henry Fielding would have been proud. His mother and father were both artists and he was something of child prodigy. He was thrown out of the Royal Academy Schools because of his dissolute lifestyle and after ending his apprenticeship with his father aged 21 embarked on a career of 'hard work, hard drinking and hard living.'[11] This had a fairly drastic effect on his health and he stayed for a spell on the Isle of Wight to try to effect a cure. He was nevertheless prolific and for the most part his work revolved around bucolic scenes of the rural poor at inns, farmhouses and cottages: subjects which were to become increasingly popular with the growing urban middle classes. Despite the commercial success of his work he was arrested for debt in 1799 and shortly afterwards suffered a paralysis that prevented him using his left hand. He died aged just 41 in 1804.

CLARKSON STANFIELD (1793–1867) ALSO HAD AN EVENTFUL life but emerged from adversity to be hailed as a master of British marine painting. Born at Sunderland in 1793, he first went to sea in a collier in 1808, four years later he was pressed into the navy and served on the guardship *HMS Namur* at Sheerness before sailing to China aboard the East Indiaman *Warley*.[12] Back on dry land he first won fame as a scene painter for London theatres including the Old Vic, but after his first exhibit at the Royal Academy in 1820 he quickly established himself as a leading painter of the coast and sea and was commissioned by William IV to paint views of Portsmouth and Plymouth.[13] *Shakespeare Cliff, Dover, 1849* is representative of Stanfield's style with its bright but naturalistic colour and elaborate composition. Shakespeare Cliff was named in honour of a passage in *King Lear* in which the Earl of Gloucester intends to end his life by throwing himself from the Dover headland:

> There is a cliff whose high and bending head
> Looks fearfully in the confined deep[14]

In Stanfield's painting, bathed in sunlight, the peak of the cliff seems to represent a divide between two different narratives.[15] On the left a brig is in distress as signified by the red ensign being flown upside down. Directly behind it dark clouds and driving rain approach: the onset of a storm that seems to have caught everyone unawares. On the beach a boat is being launched to attempt a rescue, while all around business continues as usual in defiance or ignorance of the unfolding drama. In the foreground men are working on developing and extending the harbour. The peculiar building beyond is the Pilot House, built the previous year for the harbour's pilots so that they could watch for shipping needing to be guided safely into port. In the far distance the tunnels of the London-Dover railway can be seen at the base of the cliff. With all these signs of progress the painting could be

10. Hassel, J. (1806), *Memoirs of the Life of the late George Morland*, James Cundee, p.190.
11. Henderson, B.L.K. (1932), *Morland and Ibbotson*, Philip Allan & Co., p.17.
12. Archibald, E.H.H. (1980), *Dictionary of Sea Painters*, Antiques Collectors' Club, p.202.
13. Riding, C. (2013), 'Trafalgar Squared', in *Turner & the Sea*, Thames and Hudson, p.122.
14. Shakespeare, W., *King Lear*, Act 4, Scene 1.
15. See Royal Museums Greenwich – National Maritime Museum: http://collections.rmg.co.uk/collections/objects/ 12703.html (accessed 18 April 2015).

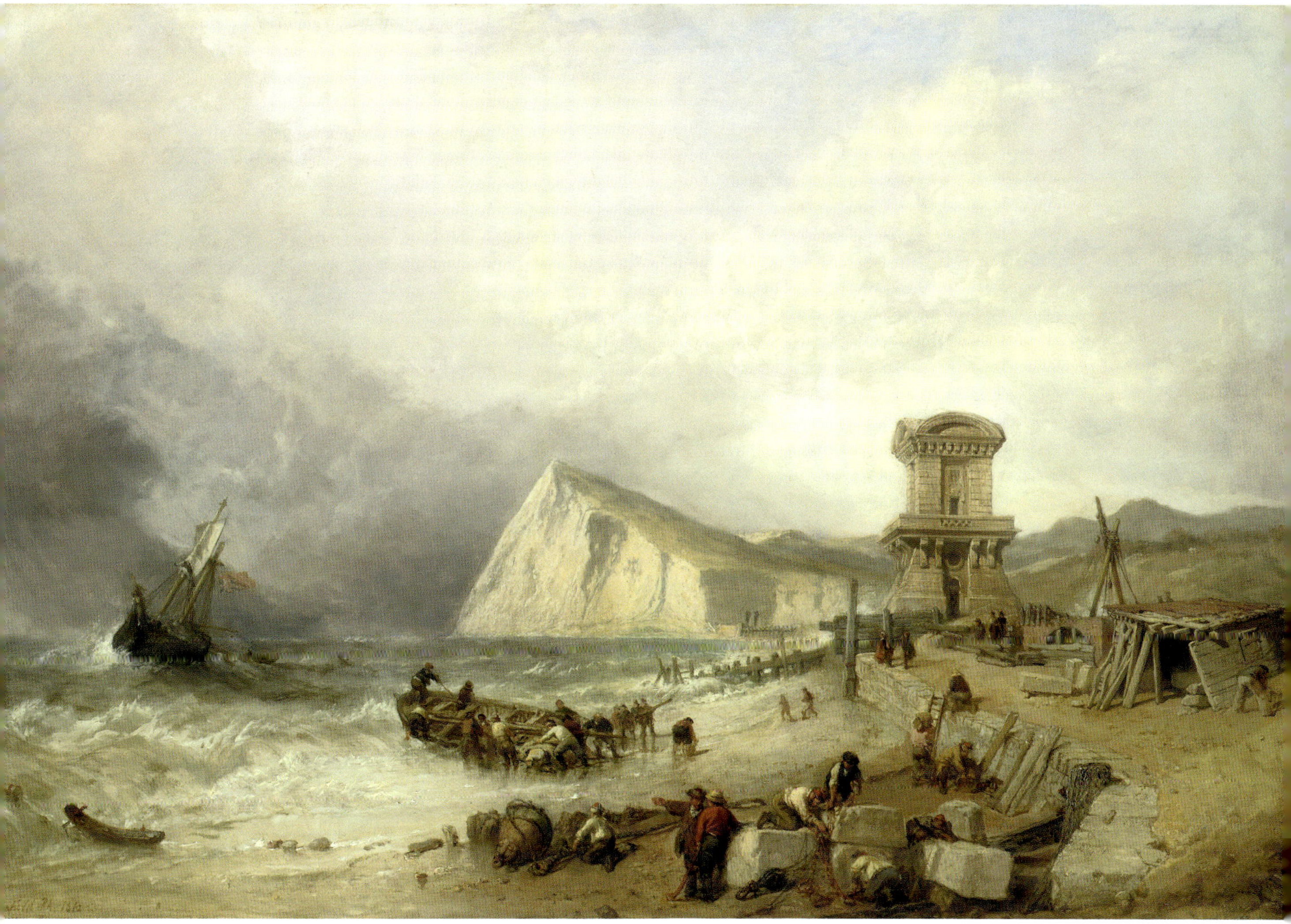

CLARKSON STANFIELD
Shakespeare Cliff, Dover, 1849
1849 | oil on canvas | 584 x 914 mm

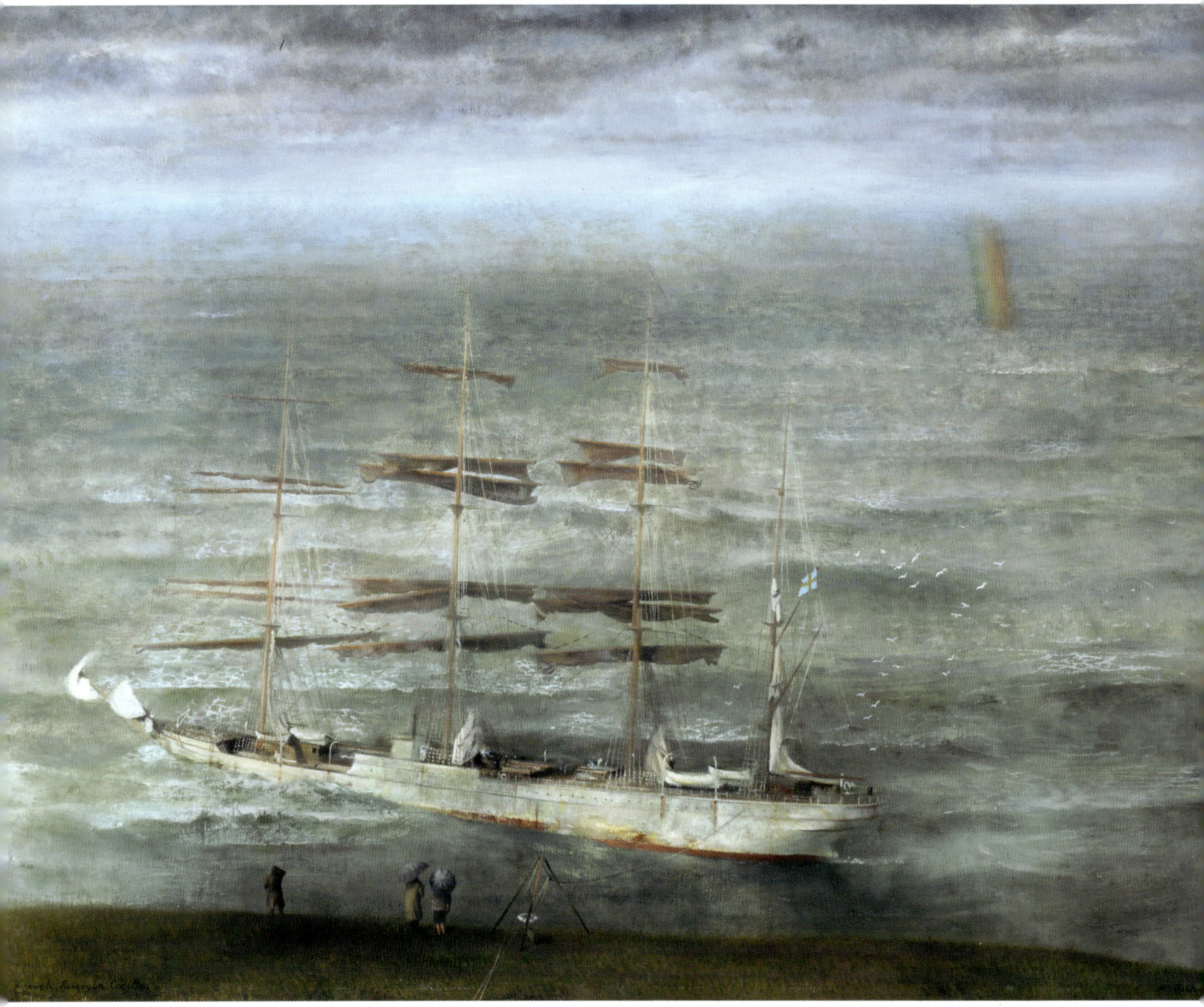

RICHARD EURICH
The Wreck of the Herzogin Cecile
1944 | oil on canvas | 765 x 1017 mm
SOUTHAMPTON CITY ART GALLERY

viewed as an optimistic statement: surely the brig and its crew will be saved within sight of Dover's famous white cliffs? However, the storm looming out to sea may have been intended to symbolise the growing fears of invasion from across the Channel in the aftermath of the 1848 revolution and Louis Napoleon's election as President of France.[16]

THE SEA AROUND SALCOMBE IN DEVON IS LITTERED WITH wrecks. *HMS Ramillies* was driven onto the shore at Bolt Tail during a fierce storm in 1760 with the loss of more than 700 men. The clipper *Halloween* was wrecked at Soar Mill Cove in 1887 with 1600 tons of China tea on board. To the east, around Prawle Point, lie the remains of the Dutch East Indiaman *De Boot* which ran onto the shore in 1738 and the frigate *HMS Crocodile*, wrecked in thick fog in 1784. This area was also a hunting ground for U-Boats during the First World War when several merchants ships were torpedoed and sunk. Even in times of peace the advent of lighthouses, better charts and navigation equipment were still not a guarantee of safety in these waters. In January 1936 the four-masted barque *Herzogin Cecile* hit the Ham Stone Rock in fog and heavy seas while sailing from Falmouth to Ipswich. *Herzogin Cecile* was built in Germany in 1902 and between the wars she won fame as a regular winner of 'Grain Races', bringing wheat from Australia to England. On her final voyage she had covered the distance from Port Lincoln in South Australia to Falmouth in 86 days, the second fastest time ever recorded. Stuck on the Ham Stone the stricken ship drew great crowds of spectators, some of whom even boarded the vessel for a closer look, greatly disrupting the rescue of crew and passengers. There she lay until June when enough of the now rotten and stinking grain had been unloaded and some of the water pumped out to free her. She was towed round to Starehole Bay and beached to await further repair and salvage work. However, in July, before she could be moved to safety, further storms damaged the ship beyond all hope of repair and she finally sank.

These bizarre events were to be the inspiration for Richard Eurich's (1903–92) painting *The Wreck of the Herzogin Cecile* (1944). At the time of its creation Eurich was a salaried Official War Artist and felt that his wartime commissions left little room for personal projects such as this. Bradford-born Eurich's first experience of the coast during a childhood holiday at Sandsend in North Yorkshire inspired a lifetime's fascination with the sea. There he spent 'four of the happiest weeks imaginable painting about seventy small watercolours and two oil paintings, never losing sight of the sea during the whole time. I couldn't bear to go away from it.'[17] Eurich first experienced the Channel shore during childhood visits to his cousins in Weymouth. He moved for a while to Lyme Regis in 1932 and painted a series of views of the Dorset coast which were exhibited in a one-man show *Paintings of Dorset Seaports* at the Redfern Gallery the following year. These pictures, made before Eurich had developed his own unique style, were strongly influenced by the work of Christopher Wood (1901–30).[18] In 1934 Eurich and his wife Mavis settled at Dibden Purlieu, beside Southampton Water, and this was to be his base for the rest of his life. It seems likely that two years later Eurich would have made the journey westward to Devon to see the *Herzogin Cecile* for himself. His preferred method of working was to make pencil drawings and notes on the spot and then use these to develop paintings back in his studio. 'The mere act of putting a pencil to paper and looking and trying to

16. Saville, J. (1990), *1848: the British State and the Chartist Movement*, Cambridge University Press, p.59.
17. Eurich, R. (undated), 'As the Twig is Bent', unpublished manuscript cited in Skipwith, P. (2004), 'Never Losing Sight of the Sea', in *Sea Change: Paintings by Richard Eurich in War and Peace*, St. Barbe Museum & Art Gallery, p.11.
18. Clearkin, C. (2003), 'Richard Eurich: His Life and Career', in *Richard Eurich (1903–1992) Visionary Artist*, Paul Holberton Publishing, p.13.

record something seen means that one has been in real contact with nature, and viewing an old sketchbook with only the slightest of drawings in it, makes a flashback in the memory which a photograph album is powerless to do.'[19] Why he might have chosen this moment to revisit sketches made eight years previously is not clear, although the rescue apparatus in the foreground and the rainbow appearing out to sea may reflect a hope for redemption as the war against Nazi Germany entered its final successful phase.

In common with many of Eurich's seascapes there is a rather other-worldly, dreamlike quality to the painting. The high viewpoint is also one that he favoured and used to great effect in wartime canvases such as *Withdrawal from Dunkirk* (1940) and *HMS Revenge Leaving Harbour* (1942). Eurich has chosen to ignore the chaos surrounding the vessel's initial grounding and instead presents the ship on a relatively calm day as rain gives way to sun with an attendant rainbow. Only three figures, protected by umbrella and raincoats, stand on the cliffs beside the breeches buoy equipment invented to lift people to safety from ship to shore. In this case it had actually been used to carry the passengers' possessions ashore and, in a throwback to the days of Morland's wreckers, these had promptly been looted by the crowds who had turned out to watch. The forlorn ship makes a rather pathetic subject. Eurich's expert rendering of the swell emphasises her vulnerability to the power of the waves and this, combined with the clifftop vantage point, lends a rather vertiginous perspective to the scene.

After the war the coast continued to provide Eurich with inspirational subject matter. He painted a number of composite scenes which drew on memories and sketches of different parts of the British coast in Dorset, Cornwall and Yorkshire. In later life Richard and Mavis Eurich would regularly make the short drive from their home to Lepe beach which looks across the Solent towards the Isle of Wight. There they would watch the weather and ever-changing light as well as the beach's inhabitants: dog walkers, bait diggers and bathers.[20] Back in the studio these observations were the subject for literally hundreds of pictures, painted with a more restricted palette and a looser, more impressionistic style than his earlier, carefully constructed work.

ERIC RAVILIOUS VISITED NEWHAVEN IN AUGUST AND SEPTEMBER 1935, staying at the Hope Inn with his friend the artist Edward Bawden (1903–89). He was seeking subject matter for what would be his first lithographic print. Ravilious was one of ten artists invited to make a large format print for Contemporary Lithographs, which had been set up by John Piper and Robert Wellington of the Zwemmer Gallery, where Ravilious had his first one-man show in 1933. The prints were intended to introduce school children to contemporary art but were also to be made available to the general public. Shortly after his arrival Ravilious witnessed firsthand the sea's destructive power: 'the storm that blew up ... was terrific – the worst here for a good many years ... The spray from the breakers crashing on the weather side of the breakwater was a quite extraordinary sight. I got very wet and I think now it was almost a dangerous walk out there, but worth it – the scene was like one of those extravagant and formless pictures of Turner's. Seaford promenade is cracked up and almost washed away, windows smashed and lumps of concrete, pillar boxes and boats and tea huts piled up.'[21] Ravilious and Bawden later went out again to watch the rough seas, but despite these experiences

19. Eurich (undated), Op. cit., p.13.
20. Bambach, P. and Toppin, C. (2004), 'Sea Pictures', in *Sea Change: Paintings by Richard Eurich in War and Peace*, St. Barbe Museum & Art Gallery, p.19.
21. Letter from Eric Ravilious to Helen Binyon, 17 September 1935, in Ullman, A., Whittick, C. and Lawrence, S. (2008), *Eric Ravilious: Landscape, Letters and Design*, vol. 1, The Fleece Press, p.239.

when it came to a subject for the print Ravilious chose to portray the harbour in a serene calm. He was particularly taken by the lighthouses which appear in two watercolour paintings *Newhaven Harbour* (*c.*1935) and *Lighthouses at Newhaven* (1935). The former focuses on the lighthouse and signalling equipment which dominate the foreground of the print, the fastidious rendering of cables, fences and architectural forms are reminiscent of Edward Wadsworth's harbour paintings, although the clarity of Ravilious's treatment makes the scene more hyper-real than surreal.[22]

Ravilious's lithograph *Newhaven Harbour* (1937) (page 30) shares the bright light and blue skies of his watercolours and in many ways the artist has transferred his method of mark-making from watercolour to the lithographic process, using hatching and stippling to create shadows and deeper tones. Ravilious's interest in pattern is evident in the contrasting textures of the sky and sea, giving energy to the former and calmness to the latter. He has also played with the layout of the harbour bringing in the left-hand jetty to create a narrower entrance. The wall on the right throws out a shielding arm, welcoming the approaching steamer to safety. The three lighthouses also emphasise the protective nature of the man-made harbour against the uncertainty of the elements. It seems probable that Ravilious felt that this bright, reassuring image was the most appropriate for the intended audience, but it is also true that his neat, slightly detached style did not readily lend itself to the chaos of the storm.

JUST AS RAVILIOUS'S LITHOGRAPH PRESENTS THE HARBOUR as a safe haven for shipping, the coast has also been a destination for artists seeking an escape from urban life among communities apparently untouched by the modern, industrial world. The artists' colonies which sprang up on the British coast in the late nineteenth and early twentieth centuries were also founded on a desire for new subject matter: dramatic landscapes and their hardy inhabitants. This exodus had been made possible by the expanding rail network which brought previously inaccessible places within reach of London and its galleries, dealers and patrons.[23] Three of these colonies were established on the Cornish coast at Newlyn, St. Ives and Lamorna.

The colony at the fishing village of Newlyn formed in the early 1880s. Its artists concentrated on capturing everyday life in a naturalistic style very much influenced by French *plein air* painters such as Jules Bastien-Lepage (1848–84) and the artists of the Concarneau art colony in Brittany. A key figure at Newlyn was Stanhope Forbes (1857–1947) who became a resident there in 1884 and was, with his wife Elizabeth, to launch the Newlyn School of Painting in 1899. His portrayals of the local working folk were 'without caricature, vulgarity or condescending prettiness' and he was 'convinced by the moral rightness of finding beauty in everyday things.'[24] His painting *A Fish Sale on a Cornish Beach* painted over six months, mostly in situ and in all weathers in keeping with his staunch *plein air* principles, was acclaimed when exhibited at the Royal Academy in 1885.[25] The Newlyn artists quickly realised the risks taken by those who relied on the sea for their livelihood. A storm at sea could have devastating consequences for fishermen and the families they left behind and this provided powerful subject matter for the Newlyn artists, epitomised in paintings such as Walter Langley's *Among the Missing – Scene in a Cornish Fishing Village* (1884) and Frank Bramley's

22. Powers, A. (2013), *Eric Ravilious: Artist and Designer*, Lund Humphries, p.96.
23. McConkey, K. (2005), 'The Pallid Gleam of the Imagination: Coastal Art Colonies in Britain at the turn of the twentieth century', in Newton, L. (ed.), *Painting at the Edge: British Coastal Art Colonies 1880–1930*, Sansom & Co., p.12.
24. Ibid., p.16.
25. Bevan, A. (2005), 'A Sort of English Concarneau', in Newton, L. (ed.), *Painting at the Edge: British Coastal Art Colonies 1880–1930*, Sansom & Co., p.33.

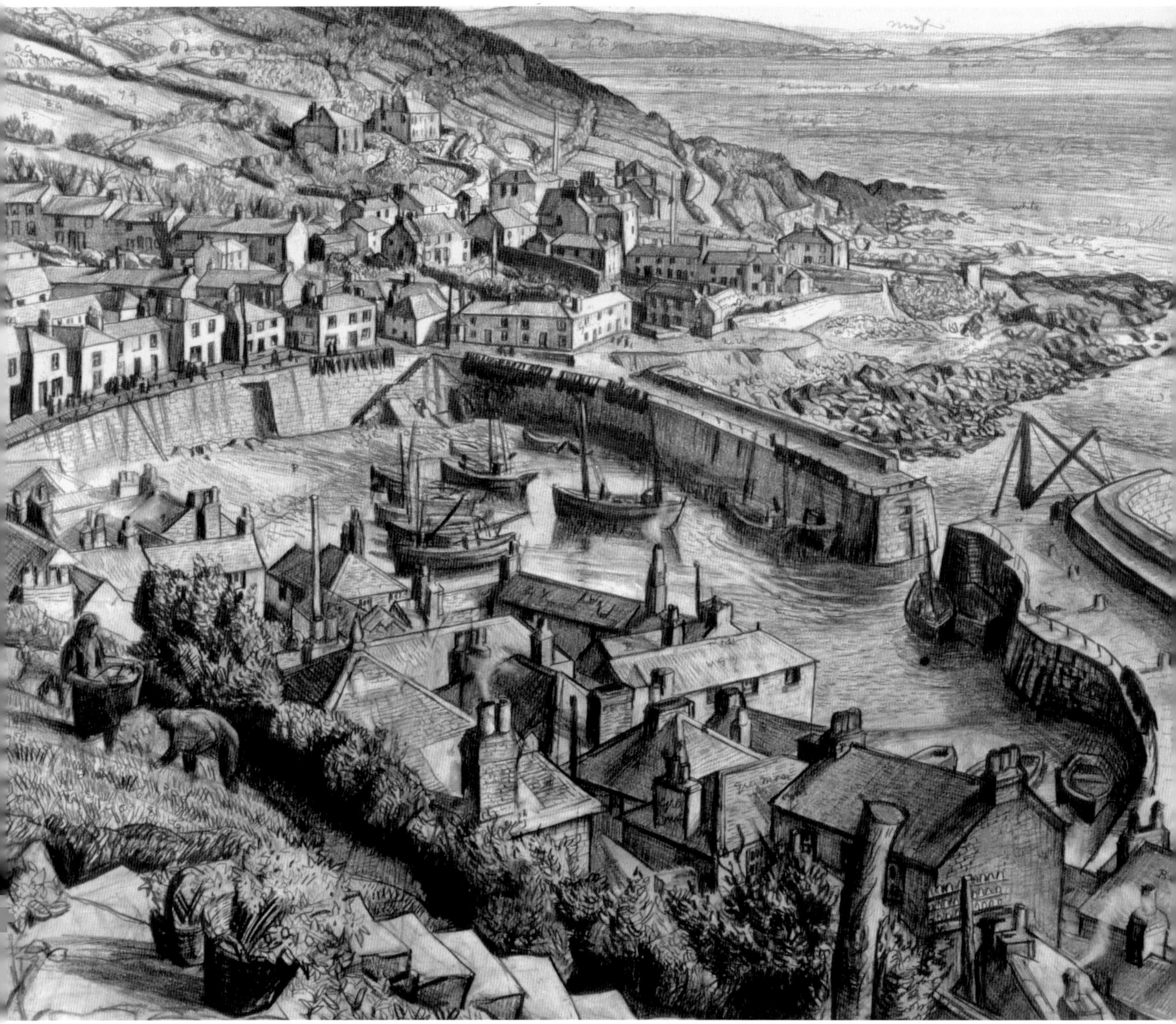

LAURA KNIGHT
Mousehole
1923 | pencil | 476 x 559 mm

A Hopeless Dawn (1888). At the same time as Newlyn began to flourish painters were also flocking to St. Ives and by the late 1880s there were more than eighty artists based there.[26] The St. Ives Art Club was established in 1890 and soon boasted over a hundred members. Of the Cornish art colonies, St. Ives was to prove both the most enduring and the most successful. Today it is particularly associated with the group of artists who gathered there during the 1940s and 1950s. When Ben Nicholson (1894–1982), Barbara Hepworth (1903–75) and Naum Gabo (1890–1977) arrived in 1939 they were seeking a refuge for their families from the anticipated bombing of London. The colony at Lamorna Cove was the last and the smallest of the Cornish artists' communities. It formed around the painter Samuel John 'Lamorna' Birch (1869–1955) who had settled there in 1892. Lamorna was five miles from the nearest station at Penzance and was the most remote of the three, its attraction lying in the timeless beauty of its secluded valley and the contrasting grandeur of its cliffs.

Laura Knight (1877–1970) and her husband the painter Harold Knight (1874–1961) were latecomers to Newlyn, arriving in 1907 from another coastal art colony at Staithes in Yorkshire 'longing for the warmth and light that we had been assured were in Cornwall'.[27] They were introduced to lodgings and studio space and were welcomed into the friendly and sociable coterie of artists. Laura Knight was quickly converted to Newlyn's preference for working outdoors on full-size canvases.[28] *Boys* (1909) showing children bathing in the harbour at Newlyn and *Flying a Kite* (1910) which looks down on the bay, are marked by a joyous brightness and energy, a reflection of her happiness and growing confidence. She experimented with painting nudes in situ by the shore and on the cliffs above, but soon reverted to clothed models perhaps in response to local disapproval.[29] Knight had been cycling regularly to Lamorna Cove to paint before she and her husband moved there in 1913. She had been given a hut on the cliffs at Carn Barges by the landowner, Colonel Paynter, who also converted cottages at Oakhill into a house for the Knights and had studios built for them. The cliffs around Lamorna Cove became a favourite setting for Knight's figure paintings: 'I knew the rocks where my hut was inch by inch, the sea there and the sky. I had studied every effect of sunlight on human flesh, determined to be familiar with its form and change of colour.'[30] The idyll at Lamorna was shattered in 1914 by two events, the suicide of Florence Munnings, wife of the painter Alfred Munnings (1878–1959) who had settled at Lamorna in 1911, and the outbreak of the First World War. Harold Knight, as a conscientious objector was made to work on the land, his stance was not appreciated locally and they left Lamorna for lodgings in St. Ives. Despite the restrictions on working on the coast in wartime Laura continued to paint around Lamorna into the 1920s. The Knights moved to London in 1919, but Cornwall's appeal remained and they were regular summer visitors until 1933. In 1923 Knight had begun to make etchings, primarily of theatre scenes, but she also worked on views of Mousehole including an etching *Drying the Nets, Mousehole Harbour* (1923) and the drypoint *A Cornish Harbour* (1926). The pencil drawing *Mousehole* (1923) has a very similar composition to *Drying the Nets* and may well have been a preparatory study. It shows the village's fishing boats at rest within the tiny harbour, their nets draped over the stout, protecting walls. Houses are clustered together on the hills above and in the foreground figures are harvesting daffodils. The atmosphere is one of restful tranquillity, a moment of calm in Knight's increasingly busy working life in London and abroad. *Sea and Rocks*

26. Wilkinson, D. (2005), 'St Ives: The Legendary Quality of Light?', in Newton, L. (ed.), *Painting at the Edge: British Coastal Art Colonies 1880–1930*, Sansom & Co., p.65.
27. Knight, L. (1936), *Oil Paint and Grease Paint*, Ivor Nicholson & Watson, p.160.
28. Ibid., p.169.
29. Knowles, E. (2012), *Laura Knight in the Open Air*, Sansom & Co., p.40.
30. Knight (1936), Op. cit., p.196.

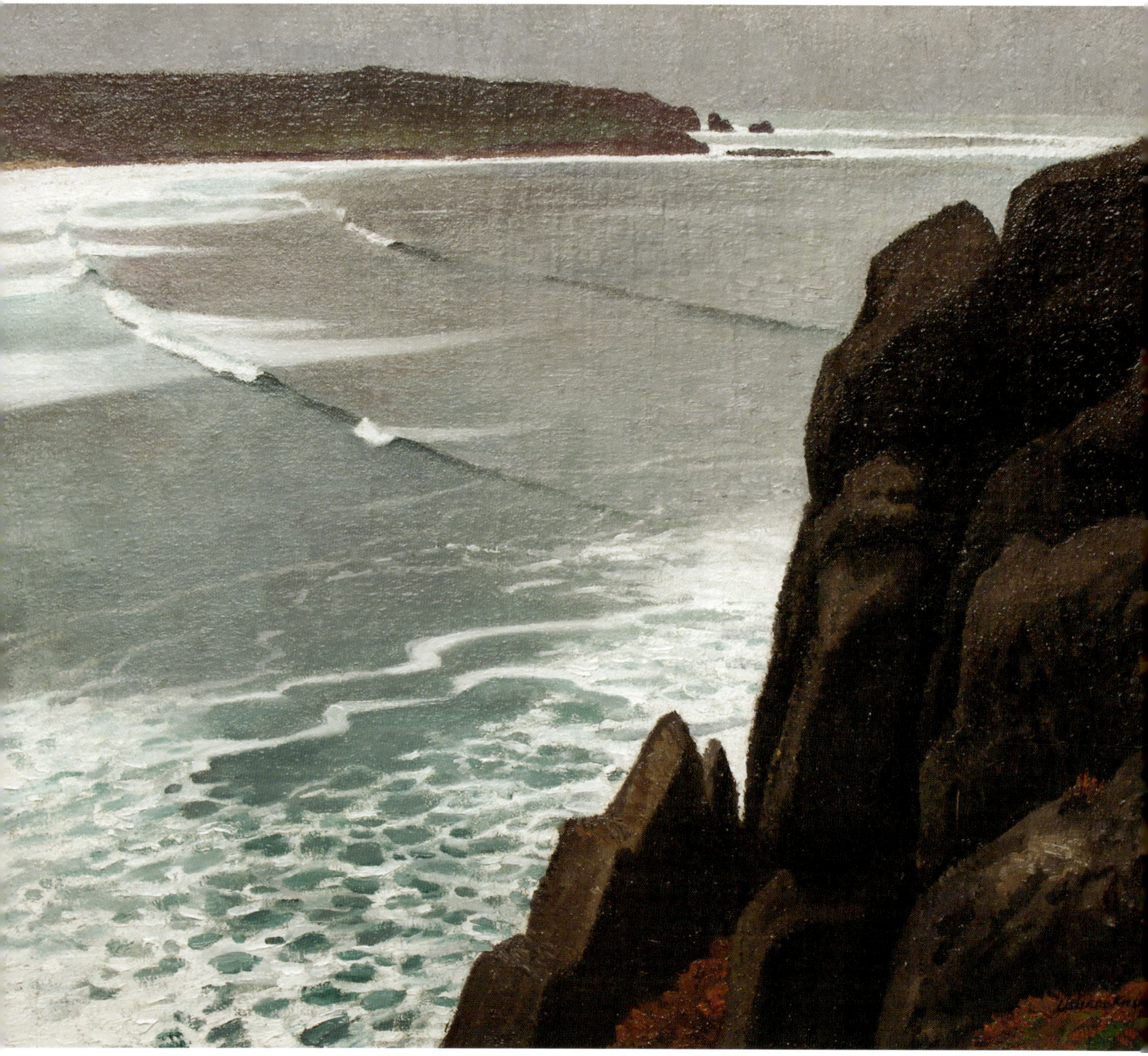

LAURA KNIGHT

Sea and Rocks

*c.*1928 | oil on canvas | 635 x 762 mm

IMAGE COURTESY OF THE INGRAM COLLECTION OF MODERN BRITISH & CONTEMPORARY ART

(*c.*1928) was exhibited at the Leicester Galleries in 1928 and was probably painted shortly before. In her autobiography *Oil Paint and Grease Paint* Knight stated 'I have a love of the granite blocks that border the coast, their poise is a study that never palls. Their dramatic possibilities in combination with the sea and sky fitted well with my mood.'[31] Certainly the dark, brooding rocks in the foreground and the grey sky reflected in the sea below are a far cry from the bright optimism of the early Newlyn paintings.

IF LAURA KNIGHT'S SLATE-GREY SKIES HERALD BAD WEATHER to come, it has certainly arrived in *Eighty miles an hour gales over the Crowns, Botallack, Cornwall, December 2011* by Kurt Jackson (b.1961). Botallack is situated on Cornwall's Atlantic coast a few miles north of Land's End at England's extreme western edge. This part of the coast is subject to the full force of storms coming in from the Atlantic. Jackson's painting is an evocation of both the frightening power of the ocean-borne winds and the rugged endurance of the Cornish coast. It displays his trademark mastery in capturing the effects of light on the water, the last sparkles of sunlight as the rain clouds drive in towards the shore. At the bottom of the canvas are the Crown Engine Houses. Their significance to Jackson is twofold. There is a sense of ownership, they are very much a part of his 'place': 'They are local to me – ten minutes down the lane from my house, so are very familiar and frequently drawn, painted or stared at from Botallack Cliff.' But he is also keenly aware of their cultural significance:

> These two early engine houses, from the mines are perched precariously on the cliff facing right into the Atlantic, but maybe more crucially they are the only really visible part of all those incredible adits and workings that go underground and even under the sea. They sit at the top of the Boscawen Diagonal Shaft, part of a once celebrated copper and tin mine that both made and lost fortunes and during the working years was well visited by Victorian tourists and even royalty: it also had its fair share of fatalities. During a decent storm the miners could actually hear the sea moving the rocks around on the seabed above their heads. As Peter Lanyon said 'these engine houses should be seen as memorials to the hard lives led by the men and women [and children] of the Cornish mining industry'.[32]

Like Peter Lanyon before him, Jackson seeks to develop a deep understanding of the terrain, ecology and culture of a place before he can engage with it as an artist. In the case of Botallack this means not only understanding the underlying social and industrial history but also communing with it as a living landscape and habitat: 'When a good storm is running and you cling to the spume- and foam-laden rock and heather on the cliff, with the seagulls and fulmars riding the updrafts and the jackdaws and choughs tumbling and battling the gales, that sense of history and maybe even prehistory is easily felt here.'[33]

For Jackson it is definitely not a case of finding and capturing a picturesque view like the artist-tourists of years gone by. It is about engaging with the landscape on both a conscious and unconscious level:

> I need to be previously informed – the physical experience and immersion comes later, with the elements and the setting feeding my mood and energy and determining the nature of the work. The location may exist as a memory from other times or be one of a series, a string of locations forming a route or

31. Knight (1936), Op. cit., p.258.
32. Jackson, K. (2015), personal correspondence with the author, April 2015.
33. Ibid.

> journey across the land. To follow a river, ancient track-way or path through the landscape slowly and repeatedly: over, across and through the countryside using the practice of making (visual imagery) is the ultimate way to discover, understand and ultimately become intimate with a place.[34]

This self-imposed requirement has been translated into a series of projects based either around specific localities, for example Priest Cove, the cliffs at nearby Cargodna, the Thames or the Solent, or particular subject matter: lighthouses, trees, quarries, mines. Once happily established in a location Jackson works in situ, often regardless of the weather, effectively becoming one with the landscape, and as a result being ignored by the local fauna which are referenced in inscriptions made on the paintings themselves. While he has embarked on painting projects that have taken him to all corners of the British Isles and beyond, Jackson's fascination with his adopted home is a constant. His choice of abode on the extreme western edge of England is a refuge of sorts: 'I feel happiest living [and working] in "marginal" places and I guess the coast is the ultimate margin and in this case a long way from the cities ... nature has a chance here.'[35]

34. Jackson, K. (2014), *Place*, Sansom & Co., p.7.
35. Jackson, K. (2015), personal correspondence with the author, April 2015.

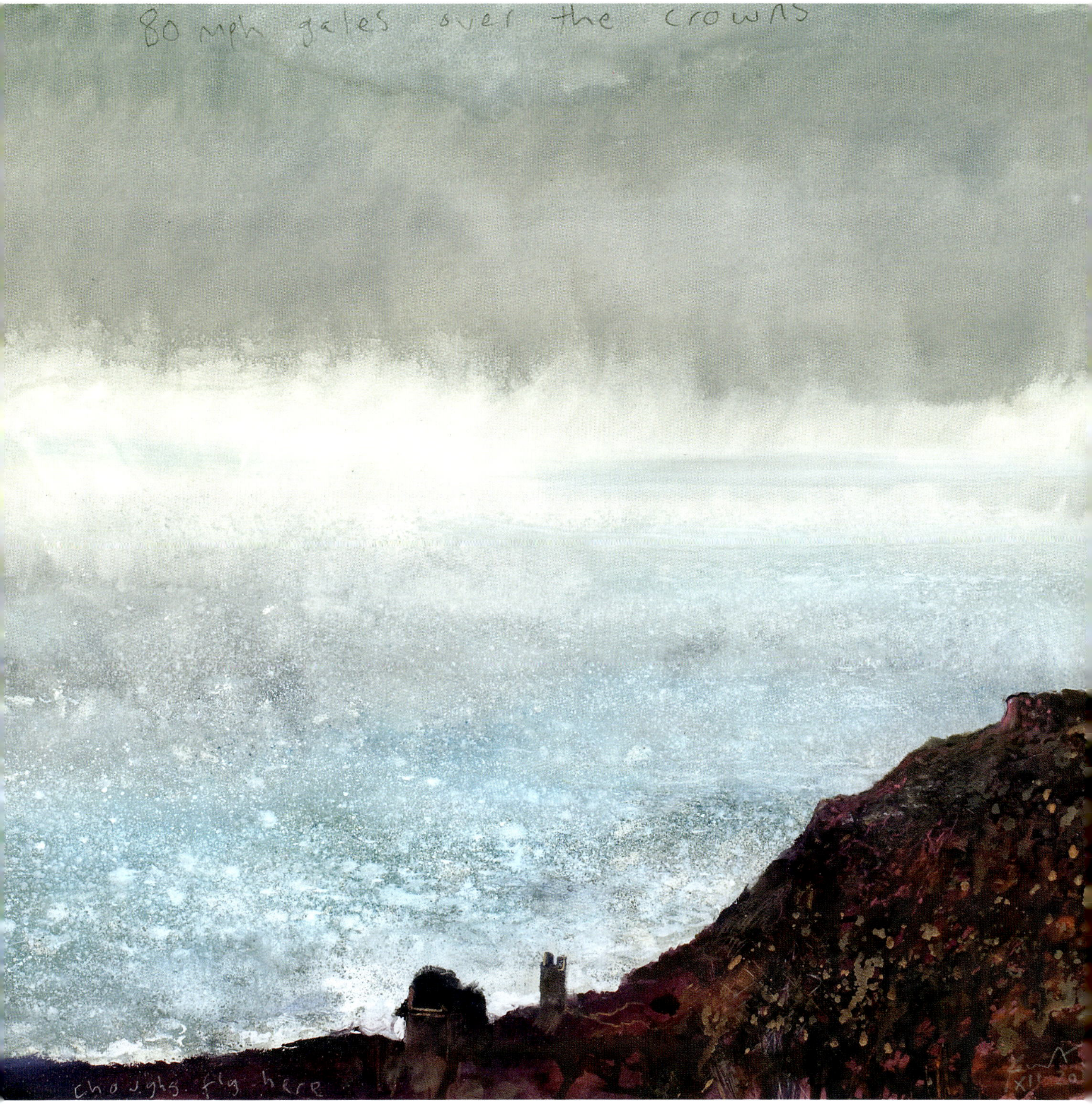

KURT JACKSON

Eighty miles an hour gales over the Crowns, Botallack, Cornwall, December 2011

2011 | mixed media on paper | 570 x 620 mm

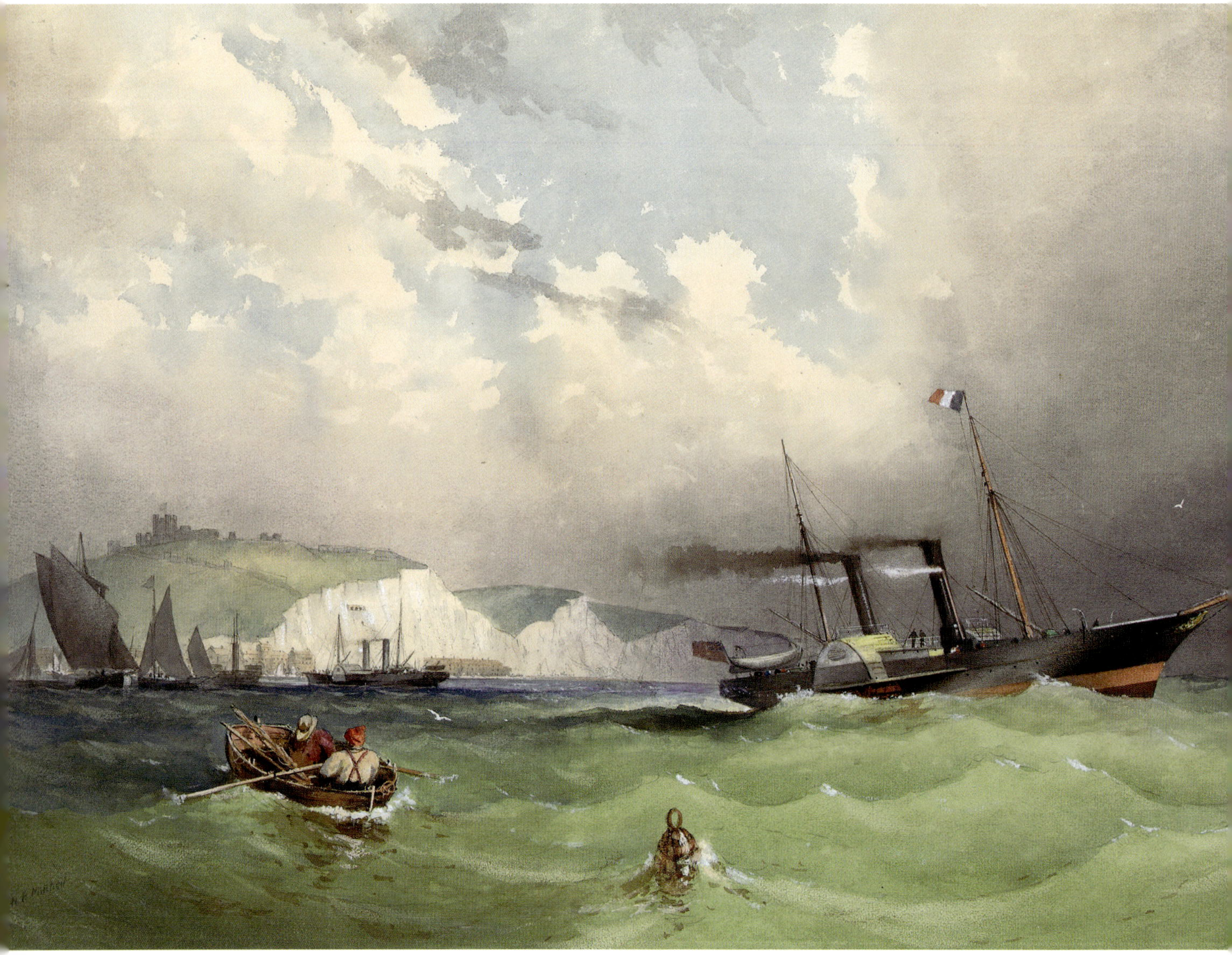

WILLIAM FREDERICK MITCHELL
John Penn Mail Packet
1867 | gouache/watercolour on paper | 517 x 737 mm

THE WORKING COAST

GILL CLARKE

'ON THE COAST WAVES BREAK AND SALT FOAM SCATTERS AND denudes, gales blow stronger and the rain is more searching ... the coast belongs to the mariner rather than the landsman. To the mariner the sea is a livelihood, but the coast is dwelling place, harbour, menace, shelter and everything else.'[1] So wrote John Piper in a seminal article 'The Nautical Style' published in *Architectural Review* in 1936. The coast in all its variety has been a magnet for artists like Piper (1903–92) who were drawn to, and inspired by its emotional intensity.

For mariners, trade was essential for their livelihoods – indeed for an island nation to prosper and flourish, trading relationships had to be established overseas, and the steam revolution of the nineteenth century had a profound impact leading to unprecedented innovation in commerce and defence. One such example was the steam packet ship, the first of which arrived in Margate in 1814; this new form of propulsion greatly benefitted the resort and others along the south coast as they made regular voyages between ports carrying both passengers and cargo.

The *John Penn Mail Packet* was built in 1867, that same year she was painted by William Frederick Mitchell (1845–1914) who depicts her leaving Dover on her way to France. The vessel was named after the marine engineer John Penn (1805–78) who had joined the family business, which was noted for its marine engines 'which helped to maintain Britain's mastery of the seas for more than fifty years.'[2] Such high-powered and reliable engines enabled mariners to trade with a degree of security.

The artist (William) Fred Mitchell was born in 1845 at Calshot Castle, where his father, a coastguard was stationed. It was in this Tudor fort that his father taught him to speak, the young Mitchell having lost his hearing as a result of contracting scarlet fever. Moving along the south coast to live in Portsmouth he meticulously painted portraits of all the major ships mainly for serving naval officers; these commissions, principally in watercolour, were the result of an arrangement he had with a bookshop called Griffins, which was conveniently located near the main gate of the Royal Naval Dockyard. Griffins also published Brassey's *Naval Annual* known for its insights 'into naval architecture and gunnery' having commissioned Mitchell to provide the illustrations in the knowledge that he would undertake them with much accuracy and attention to detail of the sails and rigging.[3]

1. Piper, J. (1938), 'The Nautical Style', *Architectural Review*, 38, pp.1–14.
2. Lambert, A. (2004), John Penn, *Oxford Dictionary of National Biography*.
3. *The Spectator*, 19 May 1888, p.22.

SEA TRAFFIC WAS ATTRACTIVE TO ARTISTS AND THE PAINTER and printmaker Leslie Moffat Ward (1888–1978) was no exception. His mother came from a nautical family based in Weymouth, which influenced his work and choice of subject matter even from a young age. In 1908, and by now living in Bournemouth, he attended the Royal Academy Schools and the local Drummond Road Art School and entered The National Competition of Schools of Art, winning 3rd prize for a design of an ancient war-galley on a moonlit sea, advertising preserved milk, and executed chiefly in purples and rich greys. The following year Ward won a gold medal for his designs for wharves and docks.

Ward was therefore well suited to the task of making lithographic posters of ocean-going liners including *Cape Liner Balmoral Castle Taking in Cargo at Southampton Docks* (1913). With the coming of the railway in the 1830s and new markets developing internationally Southampton's long, deep-water channel together with the shelter from storms afforded by the Isle of Wight, made the port ideally placed for expansion (and prominence as an embarkation centre). The Empress Dock, opened by Queen Victoria, in July 1890 allowed the largest ships to arrive or sail at any state of the tide. The mail steamer *Balmoral Castle*, was completed in 1910. The artist Norman Wilkinson recorded her leaving Portsmouth on 11 October 1910, with the Duke and Duchess of Connaught aboard and heading for the inauguration of the Union of South Africa. By the following year Southampton was Britain's premier passenger port and the so-called 'Gateway to the World' where the ill-fated *RMS Titanic* commenced her maiden voyage on 10 April 1912. The impact on the city was significant as more than 500 households in the city lost at least one family member when the *Titanic* sank off Newfoundland four days later.

The *Balmoral Castle* at 13,361 tons was the largest and latest mail steamer owned by the Union-Castle fleet, the *Titanic* was over three times bigger at 46,329 tons. Ward cannot have failed to be aware of the legacy of the disaster when he began his preliminary sketches in the Docks in 1913. The *Balmoral Castle* was the first Union-Castle ship to have Marconi's apparatus (wireless telegraphy) installed; Marconi travelled on her when she made a cruise round the Isle of Wight during August 1910 and 'made a witty speech on the subject of his invention'.[4] Ward's lithograph of the *Balmoral Castle* presents her as a working vessel with smoke billowing from her funnels and is 'Marked by strong contrasts between light and shade and a vigorous use of line'.[5] Requisitioned as a troopship in the First World War she continued to maintain the South Africa mail service while also transporting South African troops from Cape Town to Southampton before proceeding to France and in 1915 transported troops to Gallipoli. Following the Armistice the *Balmoral Castle* repatriated troops from Australia and the United States.

Ward's interest in ports and harbours extended westwards to Poole, an area he was more familiar with.[6] As a promising student he had been invited on occasion by Maud Wear (b.1873) who taught at Drummond Road Art School, having earlier spent time in Paris where she formed a keen appreciation of Post-Impressionist painting, to work at her studio in a timber yard on the Hamworthy side of Poole Quay. This waterside location 'was a critical factor in Ward's later employment of Poole Quay subjects, many examples of which feature among his very best work.'[7] *Under the Stern: A Poole Shipyard* (1919) with its subtle tones is framed by the bulk of the stern of a vessel undergoing

4. Murray, M. (1953), *Union-Castle Chronicle 1853–1953*, Longmans, Green and Co., p.324.
5. Marshall, S. (compiler) (2015), *An English Idyll: Leslie Moffat Ward – Paintings and Prints*, Sansom & Co., p.21.
6. Ward designed a number of patterns including Poole Quay and The Harbour Office for Ship Plates for Carter, Stabler & Adams in 1936 (they had taken over the Poole factory in 1921), these were adapted and painted by Margaret Holder. See *Poole Pottery: Carter & Company and their Successors 1873–2002*, edited by L. Hayward & P. Atterbury, 2002, p.57.

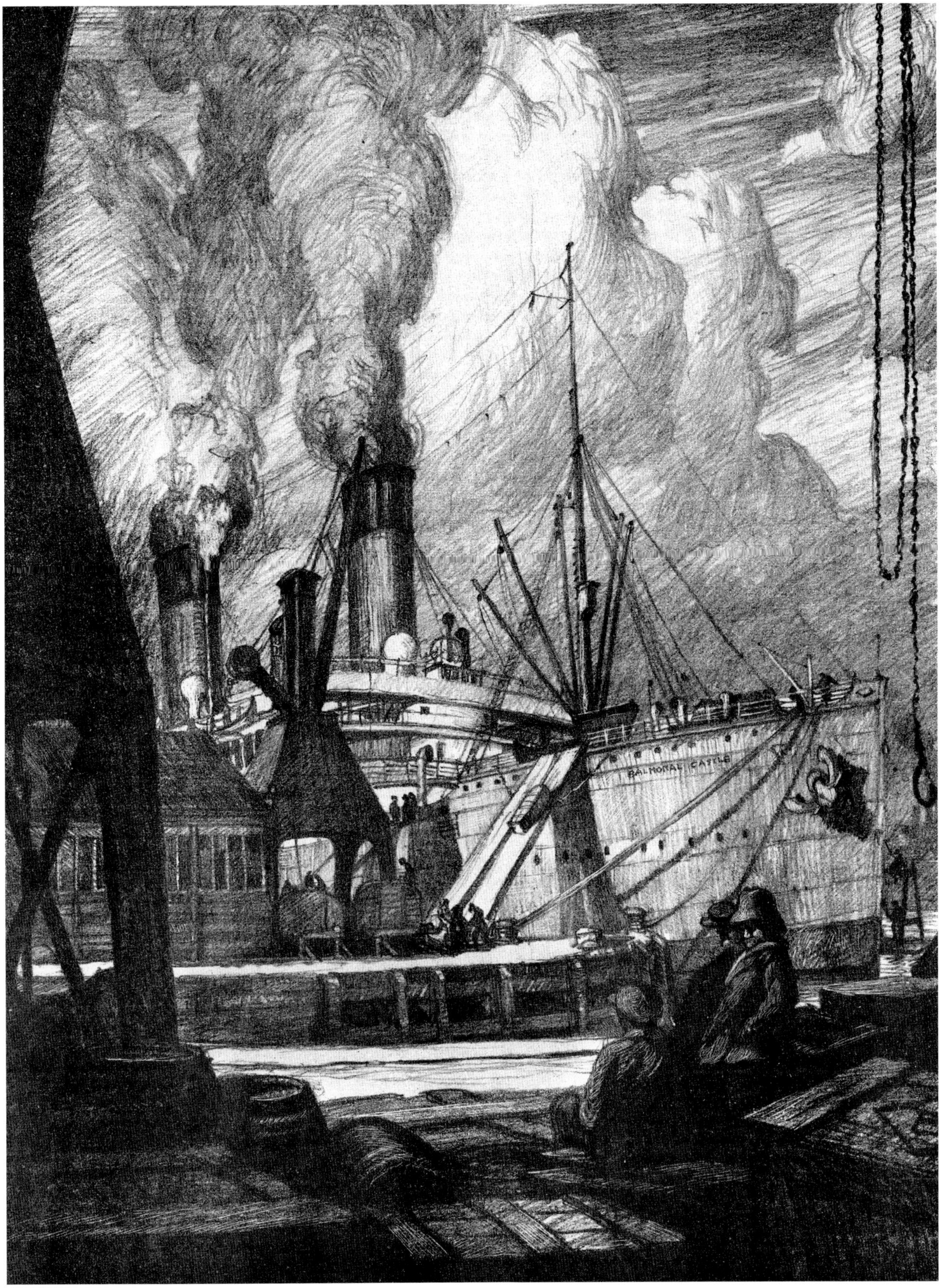

LESLIE MOFFAT WARD

Cape Liner 'Balmoral Castle' Taking in Cargo at Southampton Docks

1913 | lithograph | 442 x 334 mm

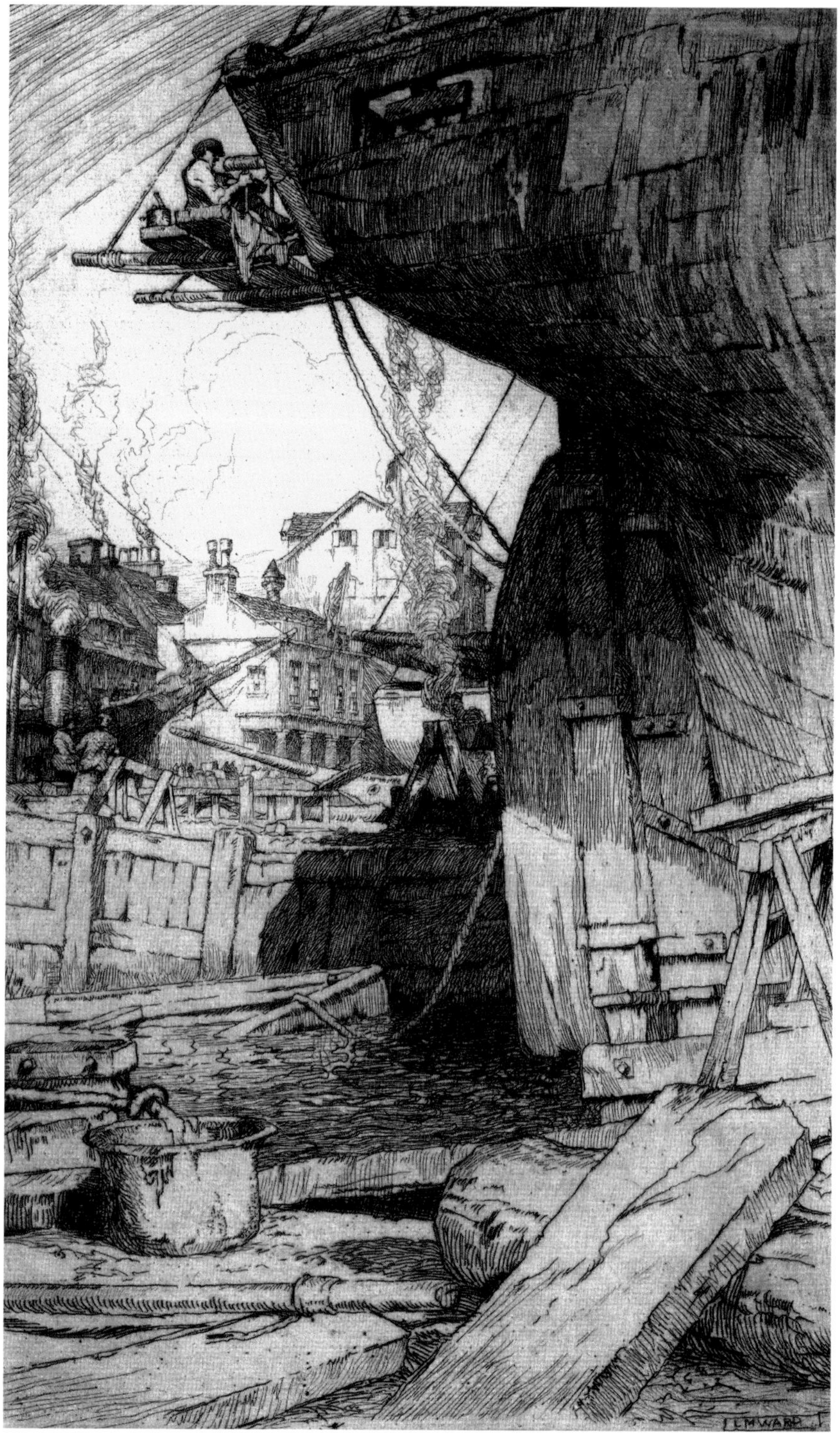

LESLIE MOFFAT WARD
Under the Stern: A Poole Shipyard
1919 | etching | 323 x 200 mm

repair. Ward captures with faithful attention to detail the detritus of the boat yard while in the background can be glimpsed the harbour and Georgian buildings on the quayside in the maritime quarter of Poole. The etching was exhibited at the Royal Academy in 1919 and reproduced the following year in *On Making & Collecting Etchings: A Handbook for Etchers, Students and Collectors*, written by members of the Print Society and edited by E. Hesketh Hubbard (1892–1957). The book aimed to be of practical value to students of the art of etching and also to collectors. Ward contributed an article on 'The Value of Etchings from a Decorative Point of View' and Hubbard, besides giving hints on collecting and storing prints, compiled a bibliography of publications in English.

Ward often returned to the picturesque Poole Harbour when not teaching at Bournemouth Municipal College and School of Art where he had taught from its inception and rose to Head of the Department of Pictorial Design. He made good use of the dinghy bought for £3 that he co-owned with close friend and fellow artist Eustace Nash (1886–1969) to observe at close quarters the vessels in the harbour. Ward and Nash frequently exhibited together and were founder members in 1920 of Bournemouth Arts Club and were often seen together in the Bournemouth and Poole area sketching and painting, taking their inspiration from what they saw around them. The artist and teacher Arthur Bell (1897–1995), a former student of Ward and later Director of Art at Cheltenham College, regarded him as 'one of a line of English artists whose main work has been similarly connected with a particular corner of the country, men like those of the Newlyn School, or Cotman and Constable.'[8] In this same tribute to Ward he commented on his work ethic which he believed followed the Painter-Etchers' motto *Nulla Dies Sine Linea* – No day without a line.

WARD AND NASH WERE NOT ALONE IN FINDING INSPIRATION in the unpretentious charm of the old town and harbour of Poole and the surrounding natural, unspoilt scenery of the Purbecks. Henry Lamb (1883–1960) for instance often stayed with Augustus John (1878–1961) at Alderney Manor, some two to three miles from Poole, the John household lived there between 1911–27 and attracted many other visitors and artists. Lamb, disenchanted with London, moved to Poole in February 1922 where he lived close to the Quay for six years in a modest early Victorian terraced house. During this artistically fruitful period his friend, and fellow artist, Stanley Spencer (1891–1959) often visited and while on an extended stay in the summer of 1923 he produced many drawings of his experiences in Salonika and Bristol during the war. Bernard Gribble (1872–1962), the well-known and prolific marine artist, also lived and worked in Poole, and was along with Lamb and John members of the Poole and East Dorset Art Society; Gribble being the first Chairman in 1924.

The artist Julian Trevelyan (1910–88) was like Ward a prolific printmaker and he too 'constantly drew on the people and places visited and ... set down whatever caught his eye ... [and] had the ability to capture the essence of a place' and while they may have had little else in common both worked with passionate concentration.[9] Trevelyan certainly caught the essence of a harbour in his first lithograph, which was produced for The School Prints project and printed by the Baynard Press in 1946. Although he produced

7. Davies, P. (2015), *Leslie Moffat Ward: A Firm Hand* in Marshall, Ibid., pp.7–8.
8. Bell, A. (undated), *Leslie Ward*, RE, Poole Museum Archives.
9. Fedden, M. (1998), preface in Turner, S. *Julian Trevelyan: Catalogue Raisonné of Prints*, Scolar Press: in association with Bohun, p.7.

a further 24 lithographs between 1946–75, Trevelyan said of the process 'it exists more on the surface, and doesn't possess, at least from my point of view, the same sculpturesque possibilities as the techniques of etching can offer.'[10] He had previously studied engraving in Paris at Atelier Dix-Sept in 1933 under its founder and director Stanley William Hayter (1901–88), two years later he set up his own etching studio at Durham Wharf in Hammersmith on the Thames and lived there for the rest of his life. He joined Hayter's Industrial Camouflage Unit in 1940 before being invalided out of the army in 1943.

Trevelyan had been invited post-war by Brenda Rawnsley (1916–2007), Director of The School Prints Ltd. to contribute to the project, which aimed to give primary school children an understanding of contemporary art. He was asked to send a 'small rough' for consideration by The School Prints Art Advisory Council, which was chaired by Herbert Read, the noted art critic, with whom he had had dealings in 1936 when he had selected some of his work for the International Exhibition of Surrealism. Trevelyan was instructed not to use more than six colours, but the choice of subject matter remained his, the only stipulation being that it should appeal to school children. The intention was to keep the price of the series as low as possible so as to keep it within the reach of all education authorities – a subscription to the series cost £4, they were eventually distributed to over 4000 schools.

Harbour (1946) would no doubt have appealed to young children and done much to enliven austere classrooms. With its bold colours, and quirky humour it encapsulates the picturesque quality of a busy, sheltered fishing port, perhaps based on Mousehole, wherein Trevelyan juxtaposes a fisherman mending his net with other characters dotted around, while several cats and seagulls optimistically eye up their 'fishy' spoils. *Harbour* like the other 11 lithographs in the series, was of uniform size 19½" x 30" including an all round decorative border of 1½" so that schools could use the prints unmounted. This first series also contained works by leading artists such as Barbara Jones who submitted *The Fairground*, Kenneth Rowntree *Tractor* and John Nash *Window Plants*. Trevelyan also contributed *Thames Regatta* to the Fourth Series of School Prints, which was issued in 1951 in conjunction with the Artists International Association for the Festival of Britain. John Piper (1903–92) contributed a mural to hang outside the Homes and Gardens pavilion during the Festival of Britain some three years after he completed *Portland Foreshore* (1948).

JOHN PIPER FIRST DISCOVERED THE ISLE OF PORTLAND, PART of Dorset's Jurassic Coast around 1929 and it subsequently became an area to which he was much drawn and this is reflected in the significant body of work inspired by this 'genius loci' between 1948–55. Coastal subjects were of great interest to Piper – he filled a sketchbook of them in 1931, and his early writing in *The Listener* in 1933 reveals the importance of such subject matter to him.[11] In 1938 he wrote on English Sea Pictures again in *The Listener* pointing out that there is no place in England more than seventy miles from the sea. He went on to comment 'The sea is a mystery that lies beyond the flat fields and the woods, the downs, the rough moors and the Black Country recesses: never far away.'[12] The Isle of Portland too has an air of mystery; Thomas Hardy, aware of accounts of the islander's skill of slinging stones

10. Levy, M. (1968), cited in Turner (1998), Ibid., p.21.
11. See Spalding, F. (2009), *John Piper. Myfanwy Piper. Lives in Art*, Oxford University Press.
12. Piper, J. (1938), 'English Sea Pictures', *The Listener*, 28 July, p.180.

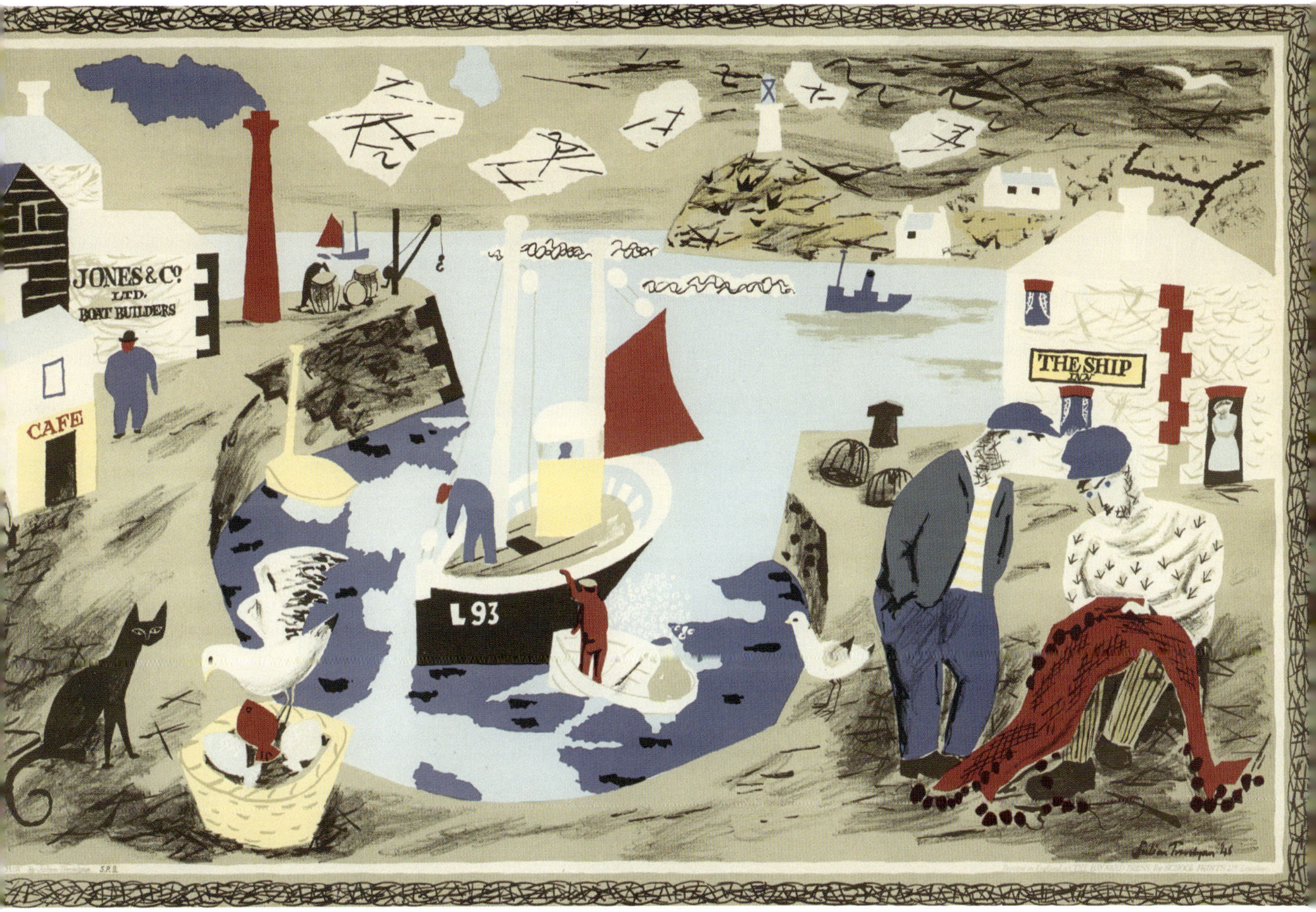

JULIAN TREVELYAN

Harbour

1946 | lithograph | 495 x 762 mm

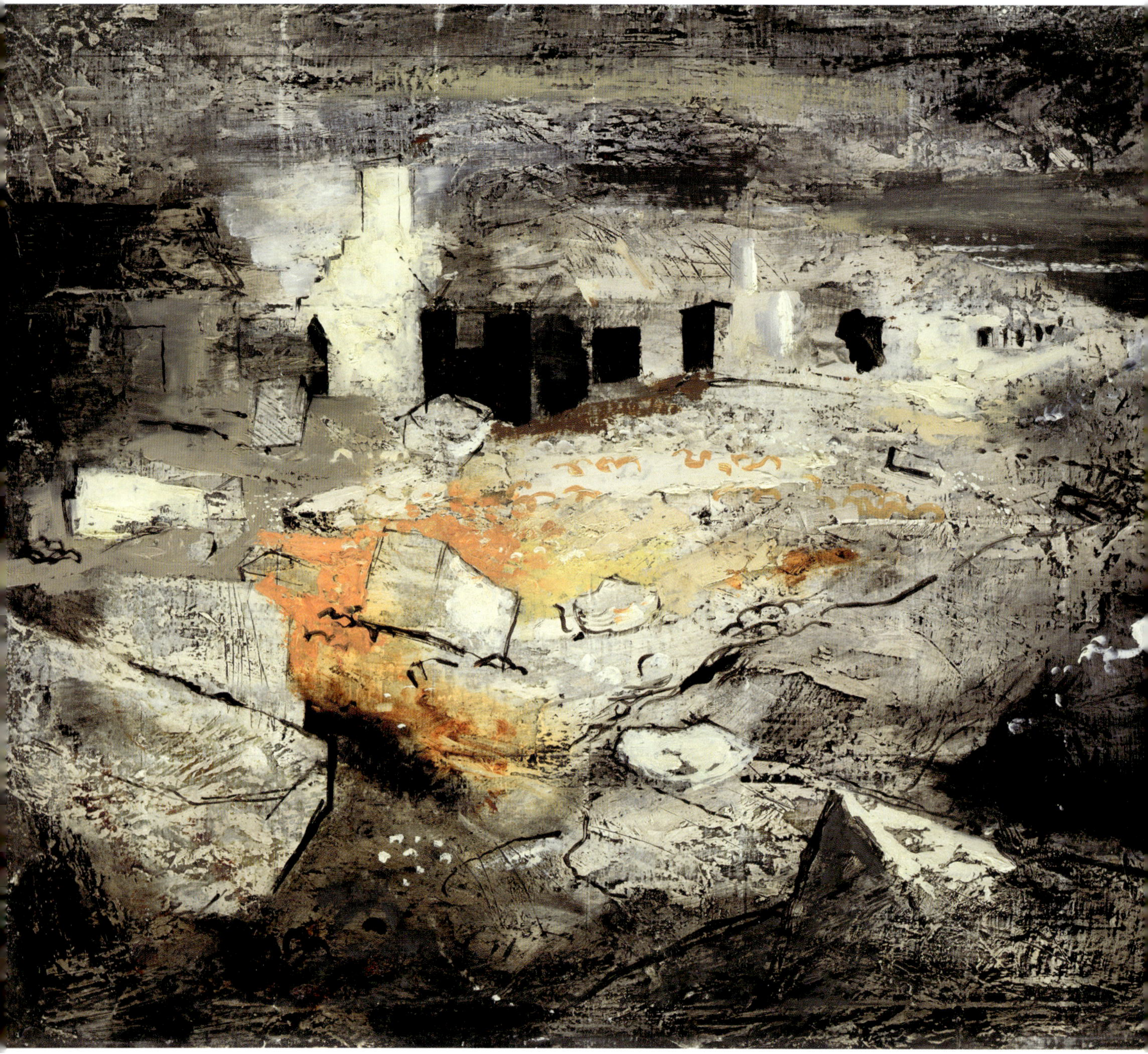

JOHN PIPER
Portland Foreshore
1948 | oil on canvas | 635 x 761 mm

at strangers to keep them away and its centuries-old history of stone quarrying, called it the Isle of Slingers in *The Well-Beloved: A Sketch of a Temperament* (1897). For Piper Portland 'seemed to epitomize all that he liked about the coast ... Though connected with the mainland by a causeway [it] is an island in everything but name, quite different in character from the mainland.'[13] It was this different character constituted by its dramatic shoreline and history with the remnants of a lost industry marked indelibly on the landscape by abandoned quarries and caves carved out by the cutting of stone that particularly fascinated Piper and which he much studied.

Piper was profiled in a BBC arts documentary directed by the pioneering film producer John Read (1923–2011) in 1955.[14] In the film, part of which was shot at Portland, Piper can be heard describing the desolate landscape, explaining how 'Great rectangular blocks, with cutting marks in regular rows, lie about everywhere, weathering in the rain and wind and odd rectangular but still angular blocks have been thrown aside, blocks whose stratification has defeated the expert quarryman, other blocks wait to be shipped from the low cliffs, and now wait for ever ...'.

Portland Foreshore was first exhibited at the Leicester Galleries in December 1948 along with works portraying North Wales, as part of a show of Piper's new paintings and drawings; he described the oil painting as an 'elaborate symbol of the place; not a view, but a history.'[15] The history is well captured by Piper, who has combined the landscape with elements of abstraction to convey a feeling of abandonment, of man long since gone. The evidence of his working presence remains on the windswept, treeless plateau which is littered with blocks of stone – the sharply contrasting earthy colours and jagged shapes make it appear a bleak and forbidding place.

THERE IS NOTHING FORBIDDING ABOUT LAETITIA YHAP'S (b.1941) *Dazzling Arrival* (1986). It is the antithesis of the sentiment conveyed in Piper's *Portland Foreshore*, there is no lament for livelihoods past but an event to be celebrated – the arrival of the fishing catch. Yhap is not alone in her longstanding interest in fisherfolk. 'The most important location for artists' studies of fisherfolk in the early nineteenth century was Hastings ...'.[16] J.M.W. Turner's (1775–1851) watercolour *Hastings: Fish Market on the Sands, Early Morning* (1824) shows his ability to observe from life and employ light and colour to effect in his rendering of a fish sale on Hastings beach with the East Parade, Battery and Castle in the distance. 'Fisherfolk were, next to peasants, the single most popular genre in the Royal Academy's (RA) annual exhibition between 1880 and 1900.'[17] Indeed, the artists of the Newlyn School, led by Stanhope Forbes (1857–1947), produced a number of acutely observed studies of the local fishing boats and harbours.

Yhap from the mid-1970s to the 90s focused almost entirely on the everyday life of the fishermen and their fleet on the Stade[18] in Hastings Old Town, East Sussex which is hemmed in on both sides by steep cliffs. The shingle beach is still used for beaching boats, with its double rows of close-set tall black wooden, tarred net-shops, mostly three stories high for storing fishing nets and tackle – there were over one hundred in the last century when the Hastings fishing industry was at its height. It was this location and the fishing community which she drew every day in isolation, and frequently in

13. Ingrams, R. and Piper, J. (1983), *Piper's Places: John Piper in England and Wales*, Chatto and Windus, p.25.
14. Read had effectively invented the genre of arts documentary films having produced the first profile of a living artist (Henry Moore) in 1951. He produced five further films with Moore and produced definitive film profiles of the key figures of British modernism, including Graham Sutherland, Barbara Hepworth and as noted John Piper. See John Read's obituary in *The Guardian* by John Wyver, 18 August, 2011.
15. Spalding (2009), Op. cit., p.332.
16. Payne, C. (2007), *Where The Sea Meets the Land: Artists on the Coast in Nineteenth-Century Britain*, Sansom & Co., p.176.
17. Lübbren, N. (2002), 'Toilers of the Sea: Fisherfolk and the Geographies of Tourism in England, 1880–1900', in Corbett, D.P., Holt, Y. and Russell, F. (eds), *The Geographies of Englishness: Landscape and the National Past*, Yale University Press, p.29.
18. Stade is a Saxon term meaning landing place.

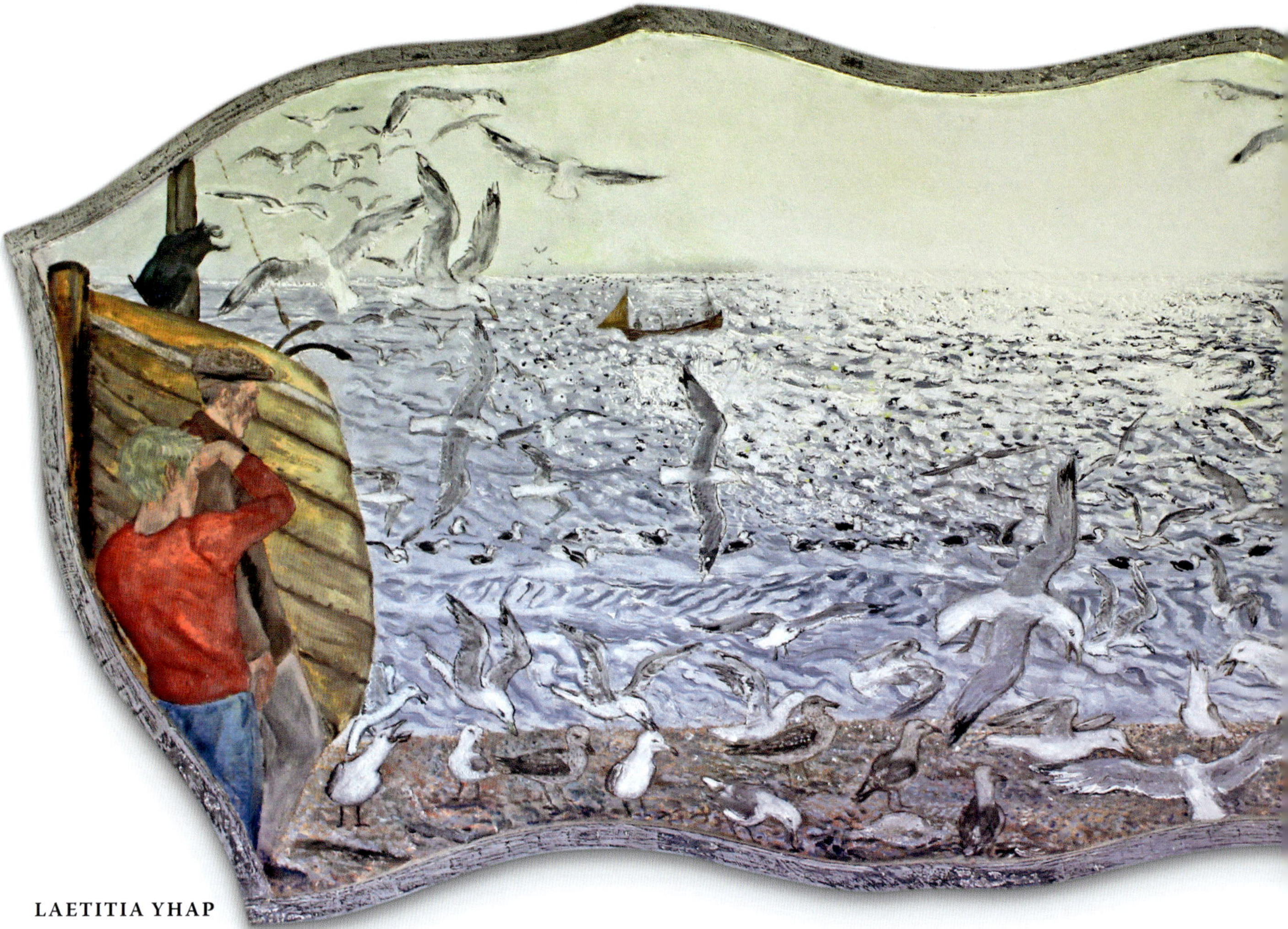

LAETITIA YHAP
Dazzling Arrival
1986 | oil on board | 686 x 1499 mm

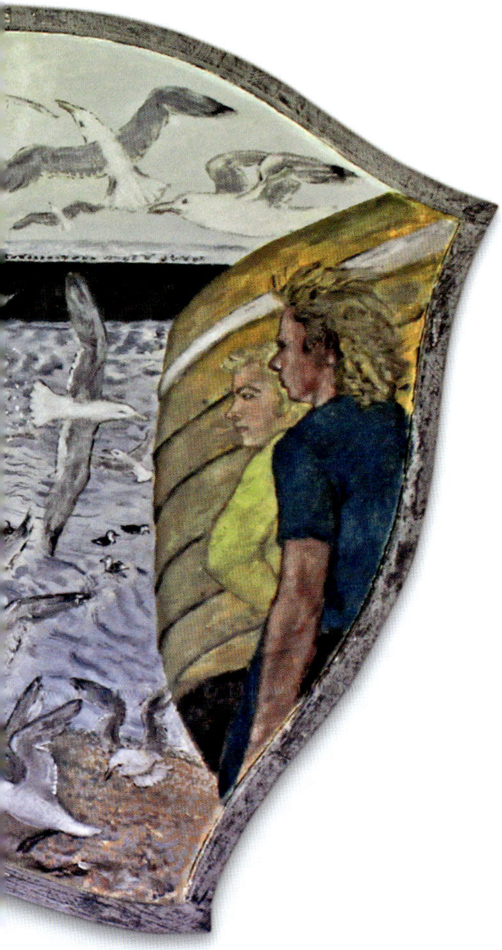

the early mornings out of doors, whatever the weather for about 18 months in the 70s, in order to gain an in-depth understanding of the workings of their livelihood, which was all new subject matter for her. As a consequence of this intense period of work she learnt much about their trials and tribulations and even the time it takes to get a boat up or down the beach and the nets hoisted in and out. The challenge for Yhap both technically and conceptually was to translate these numerous drawings into paintings. As Piper had his Portland, so Yhap had her Hastings Stade. She knew the old town well having moved to Hastings in 1967, with her former partner the artist Jeffery Camp, two years after she had finished at the Slade School of Art. The fishermen accepted her presence on the Stade knowing that she 'wasn't there for pleasure but actually on duty just as they were. They looked at [her] drawings which they often said were barely comprehensible, and began asking [her] when she was going to finish ... As things developed they had [her] doing odd jobs ... [including] painting the RX registration numbers on boats,'[19] they even took her out to sea, where she often felt seasick as the boats were generally no more than 10 metres in length so as to facilitate being hauled up the shingle (although tractors now do the hard work).

The colourful *Dazzling Arrival* was painted on wooden board that Yhap constructed, often from flotsam, she evolved her own carpentering system to create 'shapes which deliberately distort geometrical forms and which heighten the restricted sense of space in the composition'.[20] (Camp also used irregularly shaped canvases.) *Dazzling Arrival* aptly illustrates not only Yhap's unique vision and sympathetic understanding of her very specific subject matter and her ability to translate 'the daily round of their lives [fishermen] into emblematic paintings of great strength and presence'[21] but it is in effect also a realist social document that bears witness to the gradual modernization of the fishing industry. Her 'beach paintings are factual and unsentimental, rigorously controlled, and in terms of design, tightly locked together, but they are also romantic: Yhap paints her fishermen triumphing over nature. Her vision is profoundly human, at the same time heroic and ordinary.'[22]

THE FERRY TO FRANCE (*c*.1980s) BY JEFFERY CAMP WAS ALSO painted on the south coast of England, probably at Dover, some fifty miles from the cottage in Hastings Old Town that he shared with fellow artist and his then wife Laetitia Yhap (they married in 1963). The seascape of coastal Sussex had a marked impact on the work of both. Camp's work was inspired additionally by the landscape of the chalky South Downs and in particularly Beachy Head, which in an interview for the Royal Academy in 2010 he explained he loves for its beauty, and the birds and cliffs and sea and sees it as a spectacular open space, dramatic and high for a person born in flat lands.[23] Camp was born in Oulton Broad in Suffolk in 1923. The art critic William Feaver has described his paintings as 'a compendium of what he has seen, noticed, composed, modified and transformed freely. He avoids what he calls "optical" painting, the depiction of just what's there to be painted, for he believes in the freedom of the painter to create with imagination.'[24]

Described as a painter's painter Camp's lyrical *The Ferry to France* with its mastery of subdued and harmonious colours reveals something of his powers of imagination and sense of place. In the foreground close to the cliff edge and integral to the composition lies a youthful serene figure (from the

19. Yhap, L. (2013), 'The End of the Line: Laetitia Yhap in Conversation with Katy Norris', *Pallant House Gallery Magazine*, Chichester, 29, February–July, p.35.
20. http://visualarts.britishcouncil.org/collection/artists/laetitia-yhap-1941 (accessed 21 January 2015).
21. Lambirth, A. (1996), 'Laetitia Yhap: An Introduction', in *Boundary Gallery Laetitia Yhap: Maritime Counterpoint*, London, p.2.
22. Lambirth (1996), Ibid., p.2.
23. See *Royal Academy of Arts Magazine*, Spring 2010, 'In the Studio: Jeffery Camp RA'.
24. Feaver, W. (1988), 'Foreword', in *Jeffery Camp: Paintings 1949–1988*, Royal Albert Memorial Museum & Laing Art Gallery, Newcastle upon Tyne, p.5.

mid-60s Camp often placed Yhap within his paintings) but in this instance amidst some wild flowers he has placed the sculptor Neil Jeffries, a former Slade student (1982–84), with arm raised, outstretched in the direction of the ferry which is about to leave the protection of the port of Dover to cross the busy waterway of the English Channel to France. Dover had been England's main cross-Channel port for two millennia, where the first 'drive-on drive-off' car-ferry terminal opened in 1953 (and in Calais) with moveable bridges making it much easier to take the motor car to Europe: previously cars had had to be winched on board by crane. 'The opening of the Channel Tunnel railway connection in 1994 not only marked the final major development in the history of crossing the English Channel, but also the end of the ferry's ascendancy'.[25]

Camp taught at the Slade from *c.*1963–88 and during 1978–81 he stopped painting to work on completing *Draw: How to Master the Art*, a self-help manual for novices as much as professional artists, which was followed by *Paint* in 1986. *Draw* reveals both Camp's approach to teaching and his masterful draughtsmanship; it was dedicated to Laetitia but by the time of publication their relationship and his living in Hastings were at an end. The manual was well received being described as a masterpiece and the bible of all the best art students. It focused on showing ways to draw through the discipline of copying, which Camp argues every great artist did, a sentiment endorsed by David Hockney who said 'Copying is a first-rate way to learn to look because it is looking through somebody else's eyes, at the way that person saw something and ordered it around on paper.'[26] *The Ferry to France* shows us much about Camp's way of looking at the world and his ability to order that vision.

25. www.sailingandboating.co.uk/history channel-ferry.html (accessed 1 May 2015).
26. Hockney, D. (1981), in Camp, J., *Draw: How to Master the Art*, Dorling Kindersley, p.7.

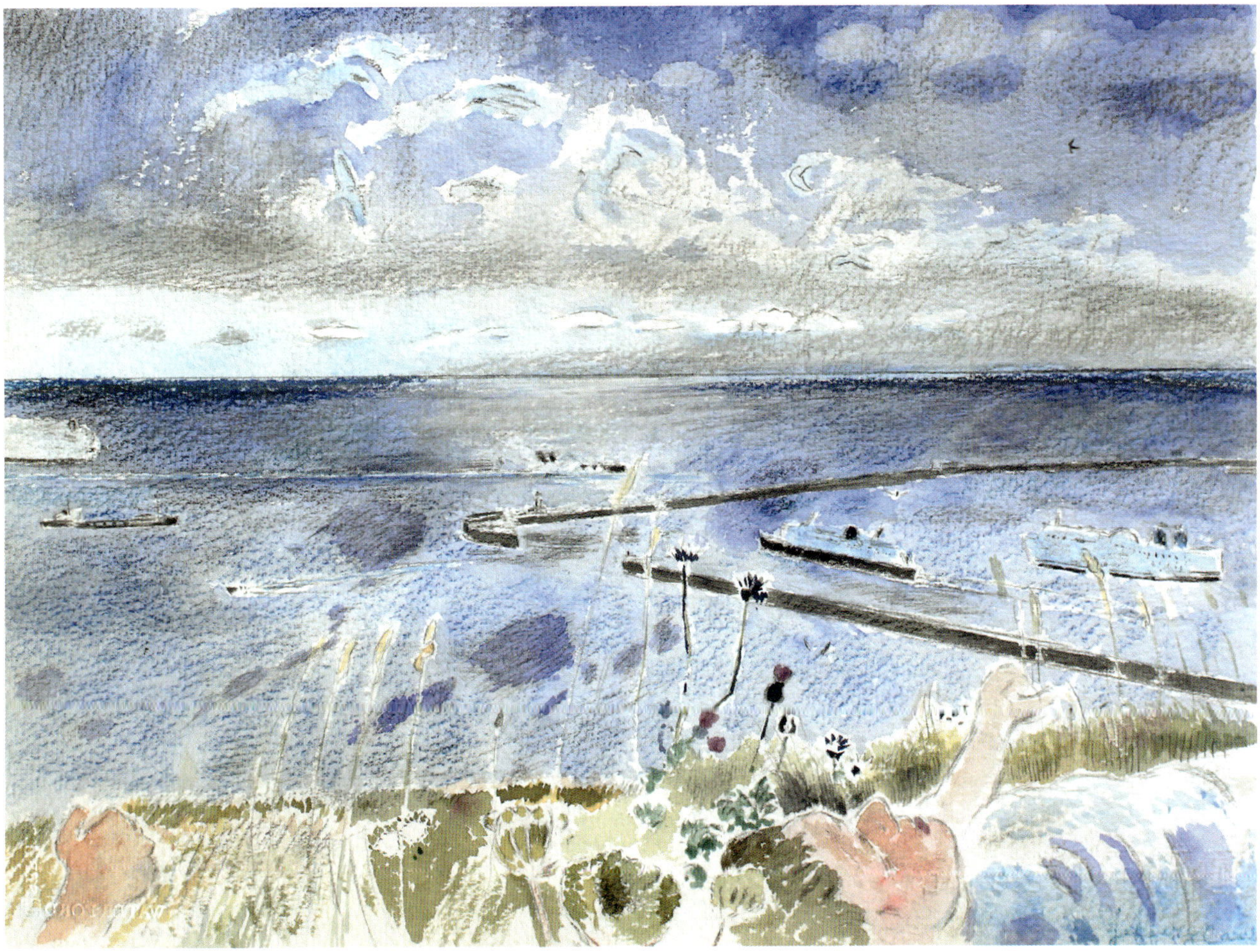

JEFFERY CAMP
The Ferry to France
*c.*1980s | pencil, watercolour and coloured chalks on paper | 280 x 380 mm

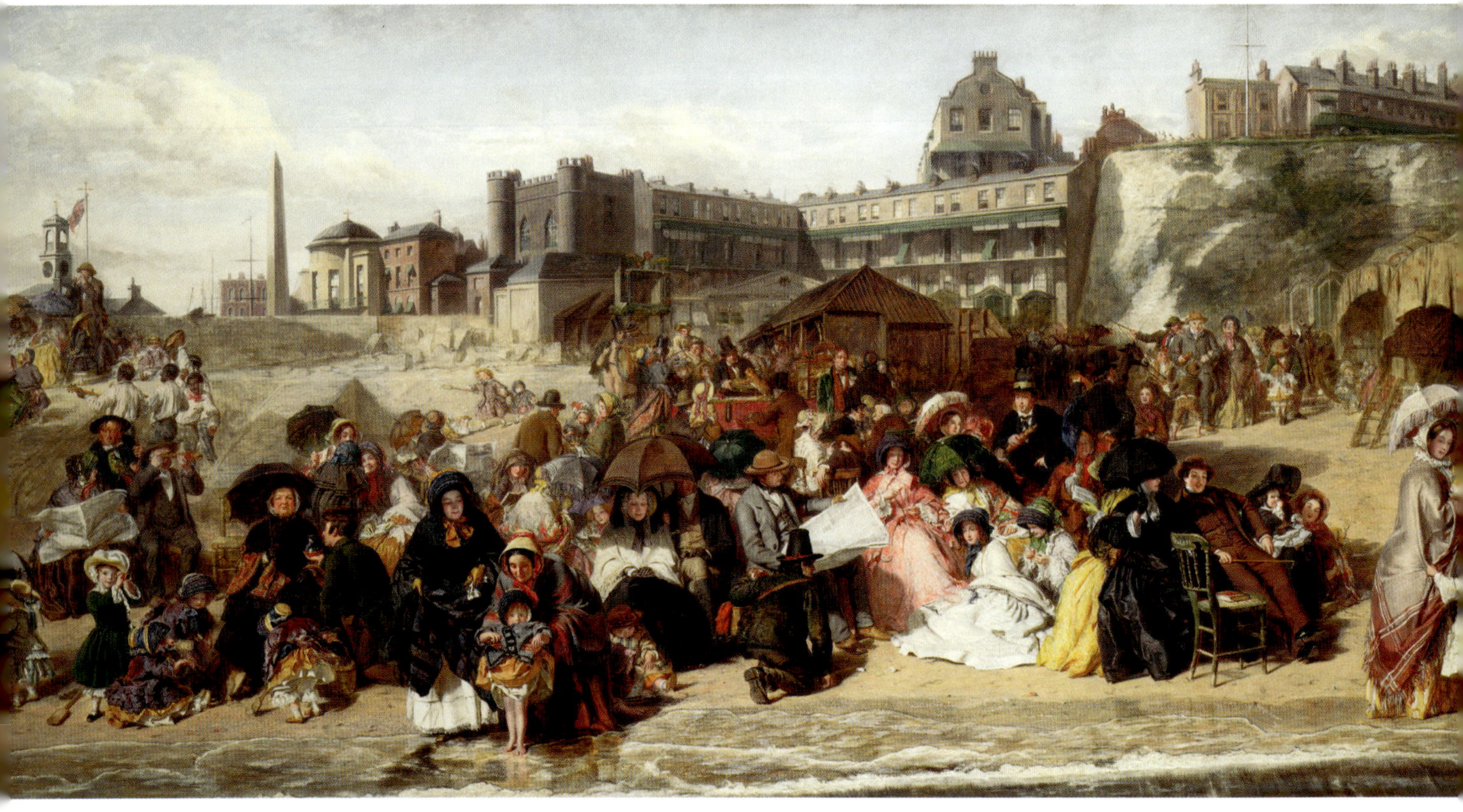

WILLIAM POWELL FRITH
Ramsgate Sands (Life at the Seaside)
1851–4 | oil on canvas | 770 x 1551 mm

SEASIDE PLEASURES

GILL CLARKE

> Until the mid-eighteenth century the sea was to our forefathers a phenomenon to be feared, accepted and, as occasion demanded, to be employed. It was to them a highway, a fishpond, a battle-ground – and a graveyard. If they lived beside it they did so for reasons of defence, commerce or transportation; they sailed it or harvested it. To them it had no beauty, no soft attractions. If they painted it it was only as the platform for some handsome vessel.[1]

All this was to gradually change as the sea became an attraction for the aristocracy and landed gentry to visit in order to benefit from the medical and therapeutic properties of sea-water that were being promoted as a cure for various ailments. Instrumental to this was the publication in 1752 of *A Dissertation on the Use of Sea Water in the Diseases of the Glands, particularly the Scurvy, Jaundice, King's-Evil, Leprosy, and the Glandular Consumption* by the physician Dr Richard Russell (1687–1759).[2] Russell who initially practised in Lewes, Sussex advocated the 'internal and external use of sea water for the same purposes as the spa waters. The sea, he said, with its four principal qualities, Saltness, Bitterness, Nitrosity, and Unctuosity, or Oilyness, seemed to have been designed by the "omniscient Creator of all Things" as a Kind of common defence against the Corruption and Putrifaction of Bodies.'[3] Such was the success and demand for his treatment that he moved his practice some eight miles to Brighton, a move that contributed to the rise of Brighton as a fashionable resort for sea-bathing on the south coast and challenged the ascendancy of the inland, genteel spa towns as places for health and pleasure. These social changes were also reflected in artists' responses to the coast and their portrayal of the new seaside pleasures that were to emerge over the coming centuries.

JOHN CONSTABLE (1776–1837) WAS MOTIVATED BY CONCERNS for the failing health of his wife Maria to send his family to Brighton from Hampstead in the spring of 1824. He wrote to his friend and one of his leading patrons Fisher, who as Bishop of Salisbury commissioned *Salisbury Cathedral from the Bishop's Grounds* (1823), to tell him that 'we are told we must try the sea'. Brighton was conveniently close to London and was now well into its ascendancy, favoured by the Prince of Wales (later George IV). Since his first visit in 1783, it had seen the completion and redesigning of the Royal Pavilion in 1822 by John Nash, and expansive building including new

1. Marsden, C. (1947), *The English at the Seaside*, Collins, p.9. Written by the former literary editor of *The Geographical Magazine* it was part of the series 'Britain in Pictures', most of which were published during the war years as an important part of Britain's wartime propaganda.
2. It had been published in Latin in 1750.
3. Pimlott, J.R. (1947/76), *The Englishman's Holiday: A Social History*, Harvester Press, p.52.

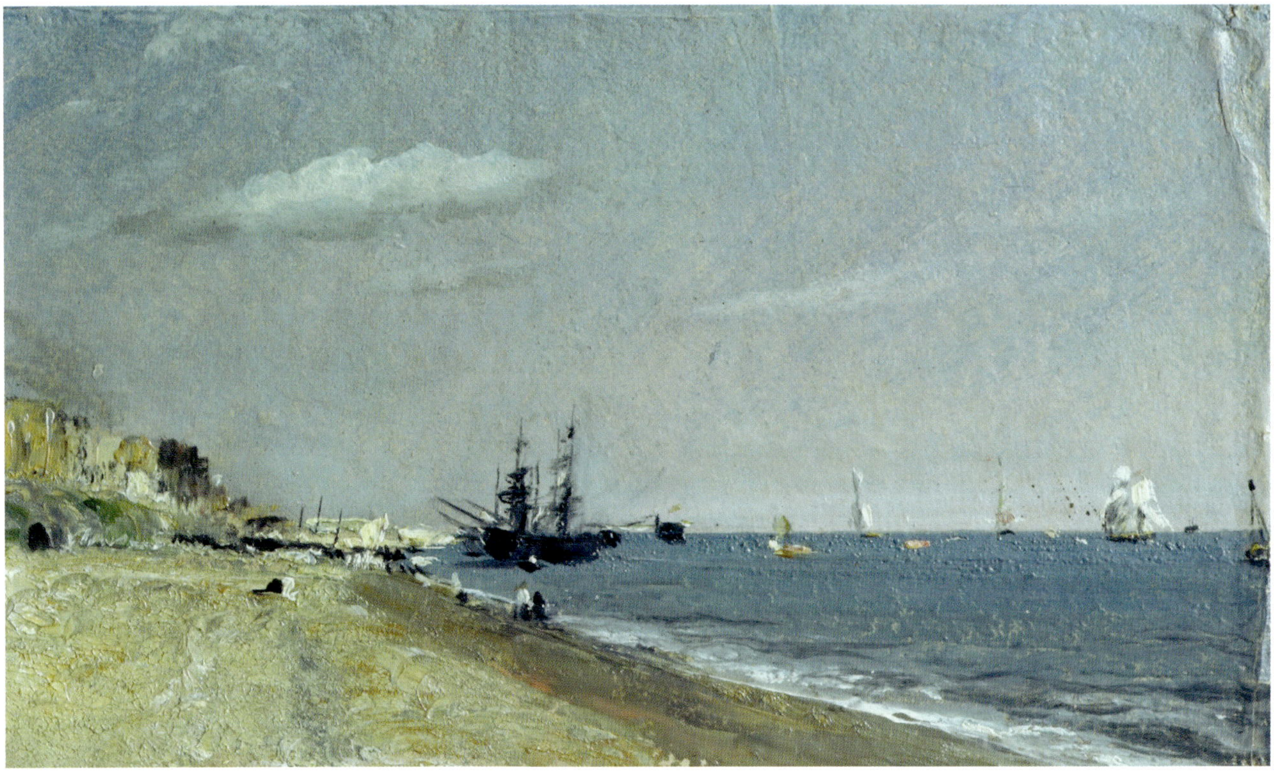

JOHN CONSTABLE
Brighton Beach with Colliers
1824 | oil on paper | 149 x 248 mm
VICTORIA AND ALBERT MUSEUM. GIVEN BY ISABEL CONSTABLE, 1888

hotels and the Royal Crescent (1799–1807), the first development to face the sea. Constable was able to make brief visits to his family, although he had mixed feelings about the resort explaining to Fisher that it is 'the receptacle of the fashion and offscouring of London. The magnificence of the sea, and its ... everlasting voice, is drowned in the din & lost in the tumult of stage coaches[4] ... and the beach is only Piccadilly ... by the sea-side ... In short there is nothing here for a painter but the breakers- & sky-which have been lovely indeed and always varying. The fishing boats are picturesque, but not so much so as the Hastings boats which are luggers.'[5] Nonetheless, Constable's stays in Brighton were to be a significant influence on his career and on his third and longest in 1824 he painted one of his small yet most famous oil sketches *Brighton Beach with Colliers*, which 'anticipates Monet by half a century, while other sketches of the open sea with only the single brush stroke of distant sail evoke Whistler.'[6]

Brighton Beach with Colliers which was undertaken on a summer's evening looking eastward reveals 'a new brilliance of colour and vivacity' in Constable's brushwork.[7] As usual he made preparatory sketches in the lid of his paint-box, which he rested on his knees. For these sketches he 'generally selected a coarse "wove" paper, which he prepared in batches by applying two or three coats of oil colour, usually adopting a pink, brown or grey palette ... These ... were then cut to a variety of sizes suitable for carrying ...'.[8] The everyday scene eschews the picturesque and shows the tide receding, the beach virtually empty, and the colliers silhouetted in black against the clear hazy sky, perhaps about to discharge their important cargo of coal into smaller vessels such as a lighter. Behind them is the recently opened chain pier which had been designed to accommodate passenger and goods traffic. It was painted by both Constable (1826–7) and his artistic rival Turner (*c.*1828). Visitors could promenade along the pier above the waves on payment of two pence and enjoy access to a reading and sitting-room and a library.

The seaside continued to attract visitors and by the 1830s Brighton was the most popular seaside resort in Britain accommodating over 2,000 visitors a week. This influx of visitors was further stimulated by the advent of the railway when journeys became noticeably quicker and cheaper. Day trips from London enabled less affluent workers to partake in new leisure pursuits on the coast.

William Powell Frith's (1819–1909) *Ramsgate Sands (Life at the Seaside)* (1851–4) (page 62) provides a well observed and detailed contemporary panorama of fashionably clad visitors relaxing, reading, chatting and being entertained on the Kentish coast while children are playing and building sandcastles. Inspired by his own summer holiday in Ramsgate in 1851, Frith explained in his autobiography that he had been attracted to the variety of characters on the sands. In the chapter devoted to *Ramsgate Sands* he described how, 'all sorts of conditions of men and women were there. Pretty groups of ladies were to be found, reading, idling, working, and unconsciously forming themselves into very paintable compositions.'[9] Photography was in its infancy so Frith had to rely on his own drawings of the wheeled bathing-machines with their modesty hoods ready to be dragged out into the sea by men and horses (in the larger resorts men also used them), their occupants attended by a dipper (bathing woman).[10] He also made detailed drawings of the east cliffs, various houses and buildings, including those of the

4. Some 50 stage-coaches ran daily in the 1820s – see Bainbridge, C. (1986), *Pavilions on the Sea: A History of the Seaside Pier*, Robert Hale.
5. Letter to Fisher, postmarked 29 August 1824, in Beckett, R.B. (ed.) (1968), *John Constable's Correspondence*, VI, The Fishers, Suffolk Records Society, vol. XII, p.171.
6. Hemming, C. (1988), *British Painters of the Coast and Sea*, Victor Gollancz, p.42.
7. Parkinson, R. (1998), *John Constable: The Man and His Art*, V&A Publications, p.25.
8. Warrell, I. (1995), 'Piccadilly by the Seaside: John Constable at Brighton', in Beevers, D. (ed.), *Brighton Revealed through Artists' Eyes c.1760–c.1960*, Brighton: Royal Pavilion, Art Gallery and Museum, p.19.
9. Frith, W.P. (1887), *My Autobiography and Reminiscences*, vol. I, Richard Bentley and Son, p.243.
10. See Anderson, J. & Swinglehurst, E. (1978), *The Victorian and Edwardian Seaside*, Country Life Books.

recognisable Obelisk in the Pier Yard, Pier Castle, Royal Kent Terrace and Albion House (the highest building overlooking the beach) where Queen Victoria had stayed with her mother between 1825 and 1836.

Frith faced the challenge of finding suitable models for his panorama: in order to resolve this he sometimes resorted to using subjects from the street or the workhouse, which caused many delays in 1853. However on one occasion he used his daughter. She appears as 'The young child being tempted into the water by her mother, left of centre, [and] is one of the most captivating characters ... and the object of her gaze was therefore her father.'[11] It's not surprising that *Ramsgate Sands* took several years to complete, but once exhibited at the Royal Academy in 1854 it was received enthusiastically, such that 'a guard-rail was installed to protect it from the crowds keen to examine the detail at close hand.'[12] It was voted Picture of the Year. Frith was the first painter to record large groups of people in modern dress, some years before the French Impressionists. He revealed in his autobiography that Queen Victoria wanted to buy 'Seaside' as she was delighted by it, but it had already been sold for 1,000 guineas. On learning this the Queen gave Frith a commission for a similar subject. However, *Ramsgate Sands* was acquired for the Royal Collection as the original purchasers, the picture-dealers Messrs. Lloyd, agreed to the Queen purchasing it from them at the same price they had paid.

The Art Union of London paid £3,000 for the plate, which had been engraved by the well-known line-engraver C.W. Sharp (*Ramsgate Sands* was loaned for three years for this purpose). The Art Union of London, established in 1837, to foster the love of art and encourage artists, distributed works of art amongst its subscribers who received a large engraving annually. 'The invention of the steel plate made it possible to produce much larger quantities of prints than before, and this revolutionized the Victorian print market. Artists benefitted enormously from this, as they were able to sell both the picture and the engraving rights for separate amounts. The print business was at its height in the 1850s and '60s and Frith was one of the artists particularly to benefit from it.'[13]

THE CULT OF THE SUN: LEISURE ON THE BEACH IN THE TWENTIETH CENTURY

BRIGHTON, AND SEASIDE RESORTS LIKE IT, CONTINUED TO attract visitors in their thousands. The Bank Holiday Act of 1871 established four one-day statutory holidays and had a big impact particularly on the working-classes who in August would often choose to make this their day out in the sun. By the Edwardian period the development of seaside resorts had become something of an industry and the arrival in Brighton in August 1905 of the first motor omnibus from London brought further visitors. Artists also took advantage of these new travel opportunities.

Spencer Gore (1878–1914) visited Brighton in the summer of 1913 and stayed for a week with Walter Taylor (1860–1943) at his house in Brunswick Square,

11. Reynolds, A. (2010), in Marsden, J. (ed.), *Victoria & Albert: Art & Love*, Royal Collection Publications, p.123.
12. Reynolds, A. (2010), Ibid., p.123.
13. Wood, C. (2006), *William Powell Frith: A Painter & His World*, Sutton, p.38.

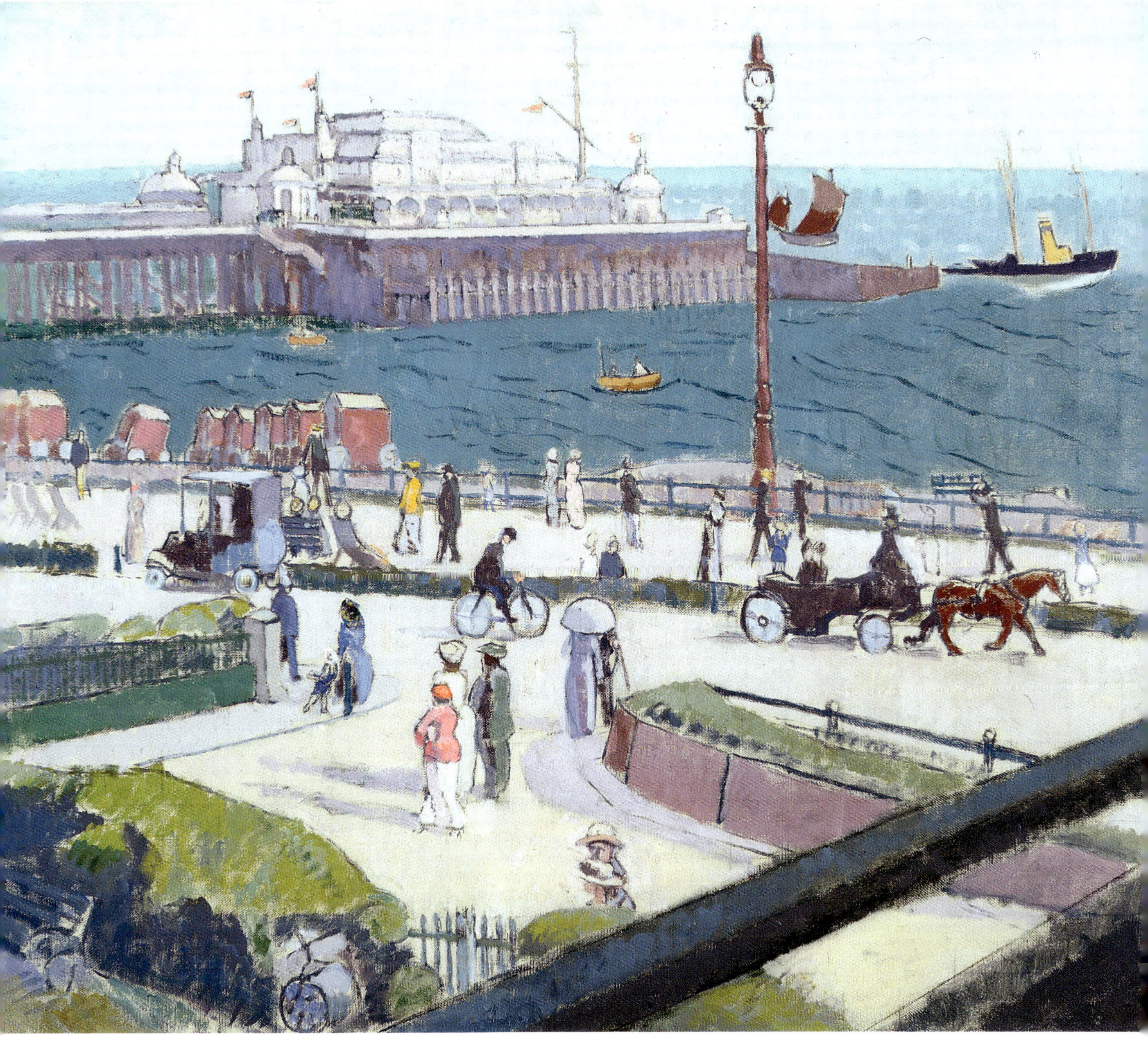

SPENCER GORE
Brighton Pier
1913 | oil on canvas | 635 x 763 mm
SOUTHAMPTON CITY ART GALLERY/BRIDGEMAN IMAGES

where he had lived since 1910, he became godfather to Gore's son Frederick (1913–2009) who also became an artist. Taylor was an amateur watercolour painter and man of leisure who, enabled by a considerable private income, studied art in Paris and at the Royal College of Art. A friend of the painter Walter Sickert (1860–1942) he was a generous supporter of the Camden Town Group, which had evolved out of the Fitzroy Street Group, and of which Gore and Sickert were founder members and Gore the first President in 1911.

Gore studied at the Slade School of Art from 1896–99 'under Frederick Brown, Henry Tonks, and Philip Wilson Steer ... learning much from their brand of English impressionism.'[14] He also gained much from Sickert whom he had first met in Dieppe in 1904 when travelling with fellow artist Albert Rutherston. Sickert was best man at Gore's wedding in 1912 and a few years earlier had loaned him his house for six months at Neuville in northern France. While there Gore took the opportunity to visit Paris and the Gauguin retrospective exhibition at the Salon d'Automne, which further nurtured his interest in French painting, his later work being influenced by Cézanne and the principles he applied. His understanding of Impressionism was also increased through his close friendship with Lucien Pissarro (1863–1944).

Gore, 'a painter who sought to distil modernity from naturalistic observation of the world, found it [Brighton] an imaginative stimulus for his work. From the first-floor balcony of Taylor's house, he completed two pictures which married his advanced stylistic vision with the picturesque contemporaneity of the subject: *The West Pier, Brighton*, 1913 and *Brighton Pier*, 1913 ...'.[15] In the foreground of the latter is the balcony railing, and neat ordered gardens, beyond which Gore has delicately executed in bright colour the quiet seafront with holidaymakers strolling or sitting relaxing enjoying the warmth of the summer sun as a cyclist pedals by and a horse pulls an open-top carriage. Behind them grouped together are a number of bathing machines, it is a scene of calm, ordered modern life. 'The picture frame obscures a numbered grid that runs around the edges of the painting. The grid reflects Sickert's influence on Gore in the careful preparation of his work and the placing of figures in their setting, belying the apparent spontaneity of the image.'[16]

Brighton Pier was first exhibited at the 'English Post-Impressionists, Cubists and Others' exhibition, for which Gore was the chief organiser and selector at Brighton Art Gallery from 16 December 1913–14 January 1914. Sickert made a speech at the opening of this progressive show at which nearly 200 works were shown from artists as diverse as Ethel Sands, David Bomberg together with the Vorticists Wyndham Lewis, Frederick Etchells and Edward Wadsworth, the English Futurist Christopher Nevinson as well as a host of other artists including John and Paul Nash, Pissarro, Sickert and Jacob Epstein.

Gore died a few months after the exhibition closed having contracted pneumonia after getting wet while out painting in March 1914. The following month Sickert wrote a moving tribute in *The New Age* captioned 'A Perfect Modern' and reflected on the life of Gore whom he considered 'became a great draughtsman by the road of colour' and 'one of our greatest modern painters.'[17]

14. Sturgis, M. (2004), *Oxford Dictionary of National Biography*.
15. Moorby, N. (2009), 'London to Brighton: The Indian Summer of the Camden Town Group', in Feigel, L. and Harris, A. (eds), *Modernism on Sea: Art and Culture at the British Seaside*, Peter Lang Ltd., p.58.
16. Coleby, N. (1995), catalogue caption in Beevers, D. (ed.), Op.cit., p.30.
17. Sickert, W. (1914), 'A Perfect Modern', *The New Age*, 14 April, p.718.

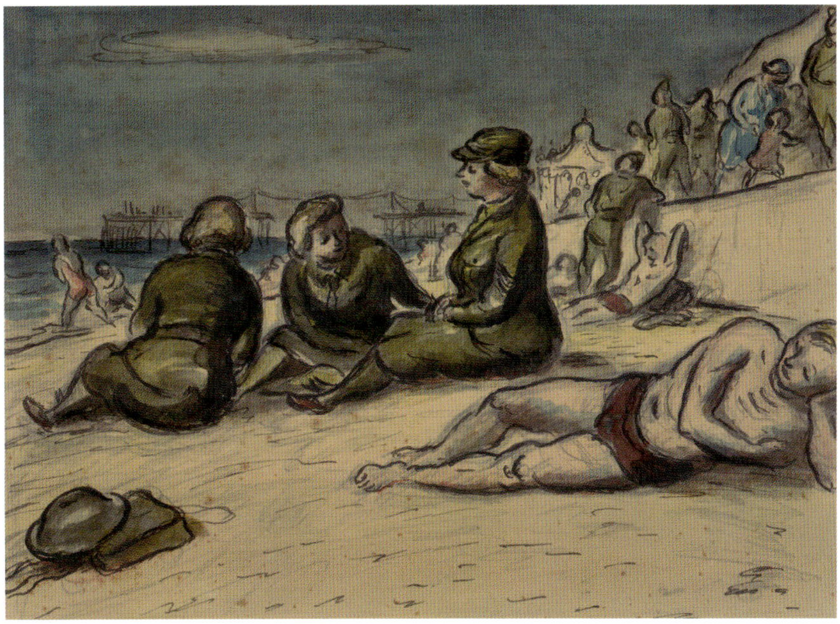

EDWARD ARDIZZONE
ATS Soldiers on the Beach, Bournemouth
watercolour on paper | 220 x 305 mm

THE ADVENT OF THE FIRST WORLD WAR SAW THE END OF leisurely holidays on the coast, vulnerable seaside locations became strictly off limits, steamboats were requisitioned and shipping suspended. The Second World War, which was truly, The People's War, saw similar precautions taken but this time piers were more directly in the front line, and in particular those on the south and east coasts where the threat of invasion was at its greatest following the collapse of France in May 1940. The fear was that piers might be used for the landing of troops and light vehicles. 'The order went out to dismantle sections of piers so as to immobilize them in the event of an attack. Sappers from the Royal Engineers blew out a centre section of most of the east-and-south-coast piers.'[18]

Bournemouth Pier, which had opened to much fanfare in 1880 (one of fourteen, including Brighton's West Pier, designed by the Victorian engineer Eugenius Birch (1818–84)) was closed for entertainment on 3 July and two days later sixty feet was blown out, on 11 July the gap was increased to one hundred and twenty feet. To prevent the enemy landing steel scaffolding was erected along the beach at the low water mark and barbed wire entangled in it. Guns along the beach and cliffs covered the gaps left near the pier – the reconstruction of the pier after the war was not completed until April 1947.

The artist and writer Edward Ardizzone had been serving in an Anti-Aircraft Battery in London where he said he was 'a rather inefficient officer in the mud of a gunsite in South London,'[19] before being appointed in February 1940 as an Official War Artist. At the end of March he embarked for France with the British Expeditionary Force (BEF). On his return with the BEF from Boulogne – he did not go overseas again until 1942 – he was sent to various parts of the country. A spell in Salisbury in June led to the production of a

18. Bainbridge, C. (1986), Op. cit., p.163.
19. Ardizzone cited in Ross, A. (1983), *Colours of War: War Art 1939–45*, Jonathan Cape, p.133.

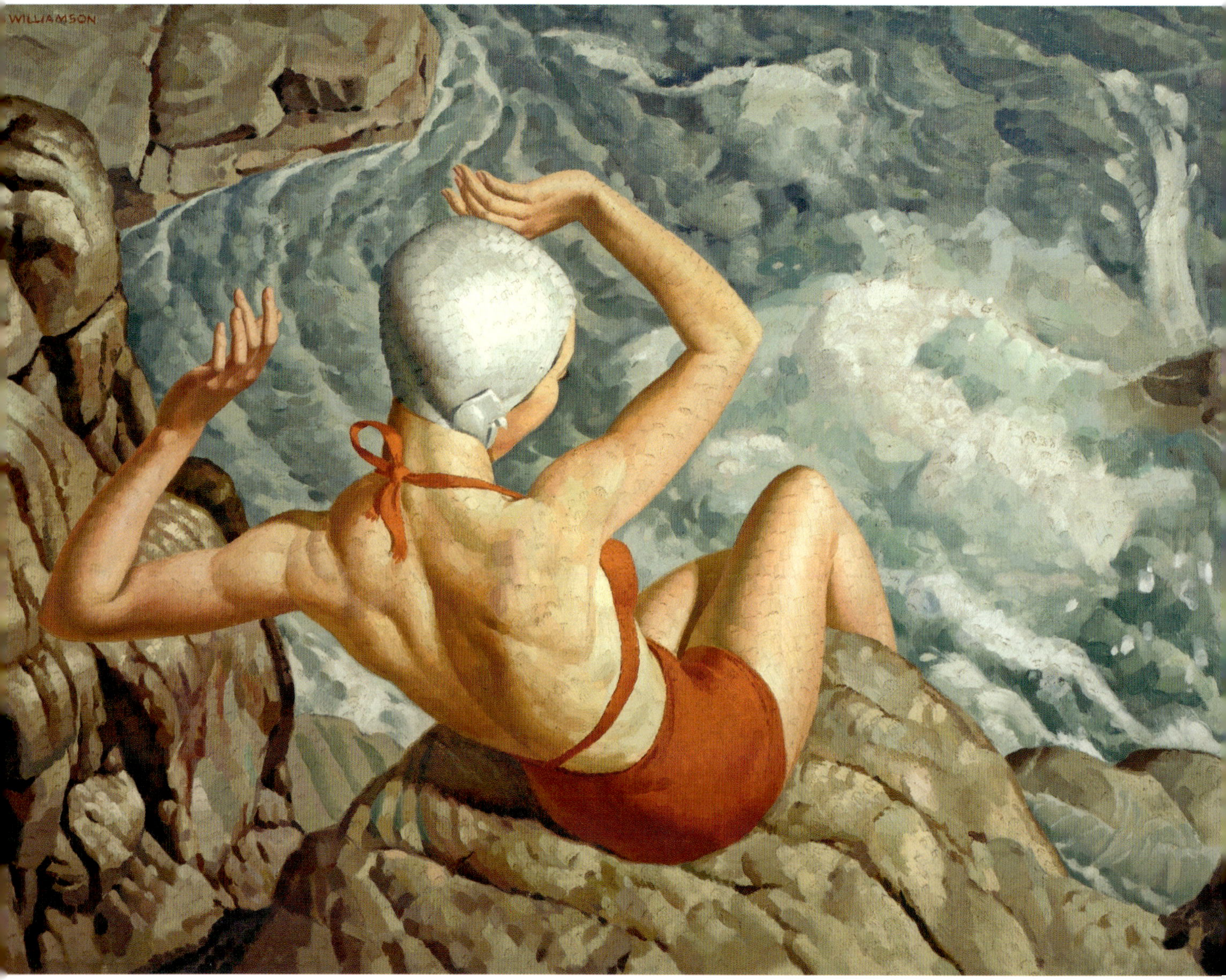

HAROLD WILLIAMSON
Spray
1940 | oil on canvas | 605 x 858 mm

number of watercolours including *W.A.A.F.s at Salisbury*; *Australians in the Grounds of Salisbury Cathedral* and *Evening by the River – Salisbury*. Bournemouth was just under thirty miles away and it is likely that during this time he visited the once busy seaside resort and made pencil jottings on the beach near the pier of *ATS Soldiers on the Beach, Bournemouth* and later worked these up on his return to base. Had Ardizzone been tempted to use a camera (without a permit) he would have found himself contravening newly imposed Defence Regulations which prohibited amongst other things the taking of photographs of the seafront and running the risk of a £2 fine being imposed by the local magistrate. Ardizzone's trademark humour and wit shine through with deceptive ease in his affectionate portrayal of three rather plump and curvaceous women from the Auxiliary Territorial Service (ATS) seated on the sand in uniform while a serviceman wearing nothing but a pair of skimpy swimming trunks lies in front of them soaking up the sun, with just his tin hat and gas mask for company.

Spray by Harold Williamson (1898–1972) focuses on a female swimmer and was painted in the first year of World War Two as was Ardizonne's *ATS Soldiers on the Beach, Bournemouth*. *Spray* was exhibited at the Royal Academy (RA), where seven years earlier Williamson had shown *On the Sands*, which featured two women in swimsuits on a beach. *On the Sands* was reproduced in the *Daily Sketch* in April 1933 under the caption *Woman as seen in the New Academy*, the critic commenting on the atmosphere of the carefree modern holiday of *On the Sands* – a situation that was markedly at odds with the privations of wartime. The Committee of the Russell-Cotes Art Gallery and Museum purchased *Spray* from the RA for £50 in June 1940 because of Williamson's local connection. The curator Norman Silvester explained in the *Bulletin of the Russell-Cotes Art Gallery and Museum* that the title was misleading. He wrote 'When you have admired the brave modelling of a young girl sitting in a happy pose, but viewed as from above (an unsatisfying view-point, making us wish it was a piece of sculpture, so that we could walk round and get a better angle) you are made aware more by the title than by action that she is in the act of avoiding spray thrown from a rock pool by a gentle swell.' He went on to comment 'Our artist is such an excellent draughtsman, so great a craftsman with his brush, and in the assessment of his tone values, that he has taken the figure far beyond the realm of dramatic movement. There are few painters who combine the art of impressionist movement with that of static form ...'.[20] Silvester was disappointed that the Committee did not also buy a nude by Williamson as he considered it the greater work of the two, he expressed this regret to Williamson in a letter on 27 June stating 'I think you will agree that, at this time, it is extremely creditable –or shall we say courageous? – of any Art Gallery Committee to purchase works of art.'[21]

The brave young model Silvester referred to for *Spray* was probably one of Williamson's students from the Bournemouth College of Art where he was painting master. Appointed in 1926 he had previously been assistant life master at Manchester School of Art and a freelance designer with the wallpaper firm Arthur Sanderson and Sons. Williamson's students greatly admired his skilful drawing of the body and his knowledge of anatomy. The swimmer's muscular back is noteworthy as is the bathing costume which shows how fashions have changed to reveal more of women's bodies with large parts of the fabric, probably the new elasticated fabric Lastex, cut

20. Silvester, N. (1940–41), 'Harold Williamson, A.R.W.A.', *Bulletin of the Russell-Cotes Art Gallery and Museum*, December–March, p.7.
21. Harold Williamson file in the Archives of the Russell-Cotes Art Gallery and Museum.

away at both the front and back. In order to keep her hair dry the swimmer wears a white rubber bathing cap. 'These caps became commonplace on all beaches by the end of the 1920s, ousting the fancy turbans and frilled caps of the earlier part of the century.'[22] Swimming, where it could be undertaken in the sea, remained a symbol of freedom during wartime, long gone were the Victorian taboos and constraints around mixed bathing, swimming was now pursued for pleasure rather than for its therapeutic value. The ban on visitors to Bournemouth 'was lifted on 12 July [1944] and the August Bank Holiday weekend saw the town flooded with people. On the Saturday over nine thousand left Waterloo for Bournemouth ... The opening of the beaches proved very popular, even with the barbed wire ... still in place. There was a heavy demand for bathing costumes even though three clothing coupons had to be surrendered for one. The shops ... soon ran out. Another shortage was that of buckets and spades for the children.'[23]

POST WAR, THE CULTURE AND APPEAL OF THE SEASIDE WITH its distinctive modes of entertainment continued to broaden with the growing commercialization of mass leisure. People were now able to take advantage of their right to a paid holiday, which had been established in law in 1938. Increased ownership of motor cars after the 1950s and rising wages, made more isolated places accessible to a wider group of consumers. This democratisation of the coast was reflected in visual publicity and in particular via railway and resort guides where a growing emphasis was placed on the pursuit of sun, health and physical fitness. Eustace Nash's (1886–1969) *Sunday at Weymouth* (*c*.1950s) captures this well and admirably illustrates in some detail the changes to the sanctity of the Sabbath and the evolving place of active and varied seaside leisure in family-centred holidays.

Weymouth had flourished under royal patronage during the late eighteenth and early nineteenth centuries when George III would bathe on the sandy beach with its easy access to the sea from bathing machines and relatively short distance from London. Nash's busy, crowded beach is the very antithesis of those of the Georgian era. Bright, casual and revealing (yet modest) and often home-made clothes were the order of the day. The beach had become something of a children's playground with donkeys (which had been part of the Victorian holiday experience), or a carousel with galloping horses to ride, and swing boats to amuse when the building of sandcastles was over. Also evident in Nash's realistic and evocative composition are changing attitudes to the sun and the open air with adults relaxing in their hired municipal green canvas and wooden deckchairs in pursuit of the sun. Deckchairs were not a new phenomenon having been introduced in Margate in the late nineteenth century, but what was new was the myriad of sun-protection products designed to enable the holidaymaker to return home with a suntan, weather permitting.

Nash knew Weymouth well having lived and worked most of his life in nearby Bournemouth and Poole. Like his lifelong friend and fellow artist Leslie Ward he had trained at Drummond Road School of Art. A commercial artist and lithographer and exhibitor at the RA he worked for a number of years as cartoonist to the now defunct weekly *Bournemouth Graphic* having commenced his gentle humorous portrayals of people and events in August 1913. Nash undertook the preliminary sketches for *Sunday at Weymouth*

22. Lansdell, A. (1990), *Seaside Fashions 1860–1939: A Study of Clothes Worn in or Beside the Sea*, Shire Publications, p.73.
23. Edgington, M.A. (1994), *Bournemouth and the Second World War 1939–1945*, Bournemouth Local Studies Publications, p.90.

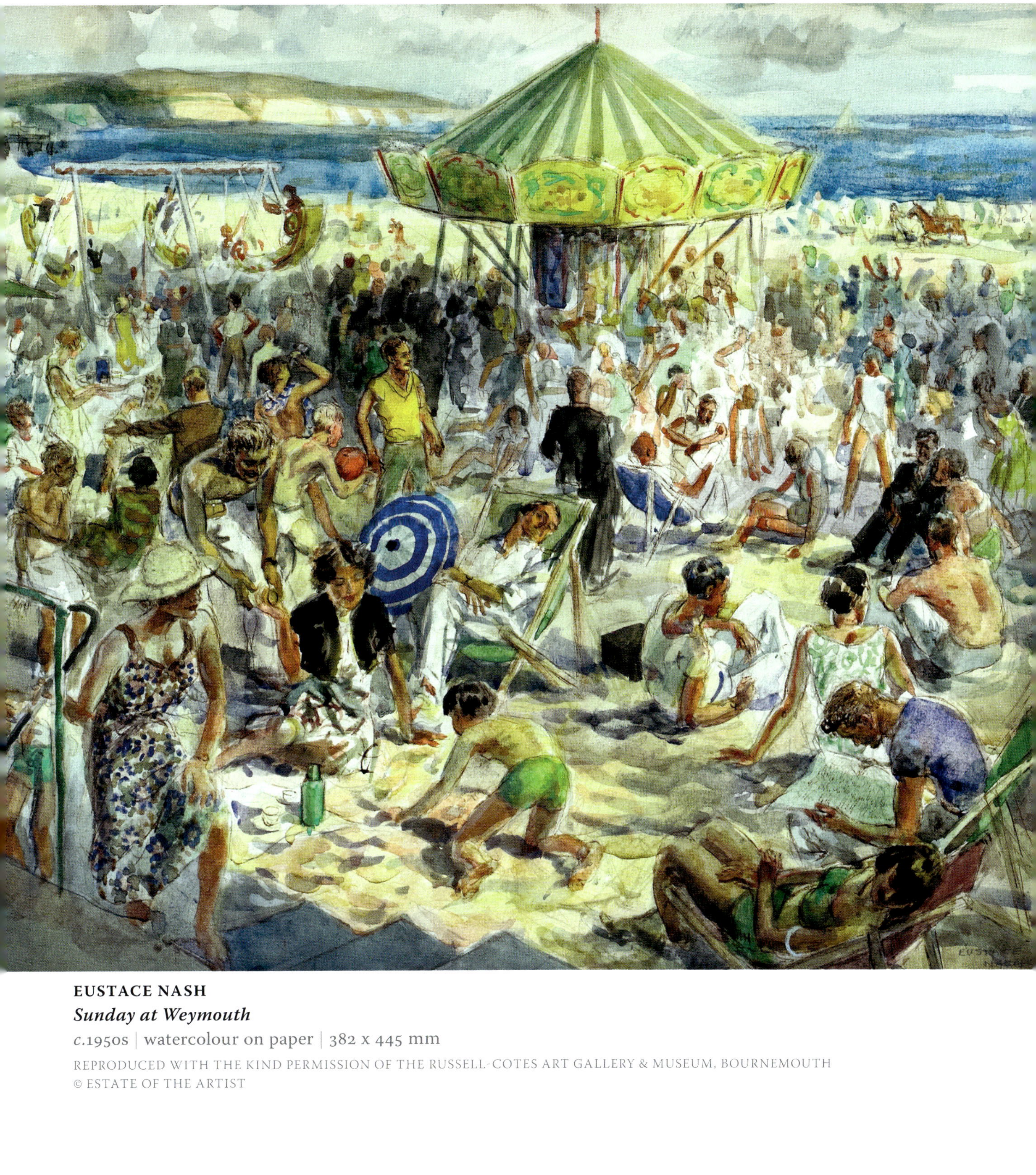

EUSTACE NASH

Sunday at Weymouth

c.1950s | watercolour on paper | 382 x 445 mm

REPRODUCED WITH THE KIND PERMISSION OF THE RUSSELL-COTES ART GALLERY & MUSEUM, BOURNEMOUTH

with great enthusiasm on a day trip by train with his young daughter Myrna. His love of the shapes and colours of the natural Dorset scene and the impact of light and shadow on these inspired the painting.

Conspicuous by his absence from the seaside scene is the ubiquitous Punch and Judy showman Frank Edmonds, who had performed in all weathers on the Weymouth beach for some fifty years. Stephen Bone (1904–58) on a seaside painting trip in 1946, most likely with his father the artist Sir Muirhead Bone (1876–1953), from his cottage near Lymington recorded *Punch at Weymouth*. It was exhibited at the Leicester Galleries and reproduced in *The Listener* on 12 December 1946 and shows a windswept and rather empty beach which was in sharp contrast to the sun-drenched and crowded sands of Nash's *Sunday at Weymouth*. Elsewhere Punch and Judy appears in *July, the Seaside* by Laurence Stephen Lowry (1943) and Ardizzone drew Punch and Judy at Whitestone Pond on Hampstead Heath in 1955. Frith's much earlier painting *Ramsgate Sands (Life at the Seaside)* (1851–4) includes an ornate Punch and Judy booth on the middle of the sands and some twenty-three years earlier the well-known caricaturist George Cruikshank (1792–1878) illustrated the first printed Punch and Judy script by John Payne Collier.

PUNCH AND JUDY WAS ALSO A REGULAR SUMMER FEATURE further eastward from Weymouth, on Swanage beach. Percival (Percy) Wise's (1883–1968) *Punch and Judy on Swanage Beach* (1962) records Ernest Brisbane who had performed at the Festival of Britain in 1951[24] entertaining a crowd of young children enjoying the antics of Punch. Wise knew Nash well as both were actively involved in the art scene in Bournemouth and Poole. Wise had served on the organising committee of the Poole and East Dorset Art Society since 1926 and later he was elected Acting Vice President with the marine artist Bernard Gribble, whose work he much admired. After Gribble's death in 1962 Wise succeeded him as chairman. 'Many of their members worked in a style loosely based on the bright colours and free brushwork of the French Impressionist and Post-Impressionist painters.'[25] Wise had moved to Dorset in 1925 to take up the post of Headmaster of Poole School of Art, a post he held until retirement in 1946; previously he had been Head of Carmarthen School of Arts and Crafts in South Wales. As Headmaster Wise met and knew many other working artists including Henry Lamb who lived close to the art school and who attended the life classes so as to use the model. On other occasions Lamb would cycle to Wise's house and they would discuss art and music.[26]

Punch and Judy on Swanage Beach was undertaken well into Wise's retirement when he was aged 77 and probably begun on a summer holiday in 1961. As he did not own a car or drive he most likely took the bus or train to Swanage. Further, given it was 'impractical to carry large wet canvasses around on field trips ... he would bring his work home in one of those old Barkers' trunks, used by children to take to boarding school' and which could be sent in advance to a holiday destination.[27] He would no doubt have taken the opportunity to make numerous annotated watercolours to use as aides memoires for his final oil painting of Punch and Judy together with a photograph or two. Wise had a deep love of the natural environment and his adopted county of Dorset and Swanage in particular. Paul Nash had also much enjoyed his stay in Swanage but with rather different artistic results.

24. See Stinton, J. (2012), *The Way to Do It: Frank Edmonds, Punch & Judy Man*, Harlequin Press. The South Bank Exhibition during the Festival of Britain (1951) contained a number of Pavilions that related to the coast. Of one titled Seaside the description stated 'Our maritime character as expressed at home – the port, the seaside resort, the wild coastline between them.'
25. *Discovering Poole: An Artist's Haven 1850–1950*, Poole Museum Service (2009), unpaginated.
26. See *Percival A Wise ARCA FRSA: His life and Work (1883–1968)*, unpublished BA (Hons) Graphic Design/Illustration thesis by Kevin Dempsey (1990), Brighton Polytechnic, Poole Museum Archives.
27. Dempsey (1990), Ibid., p.45.

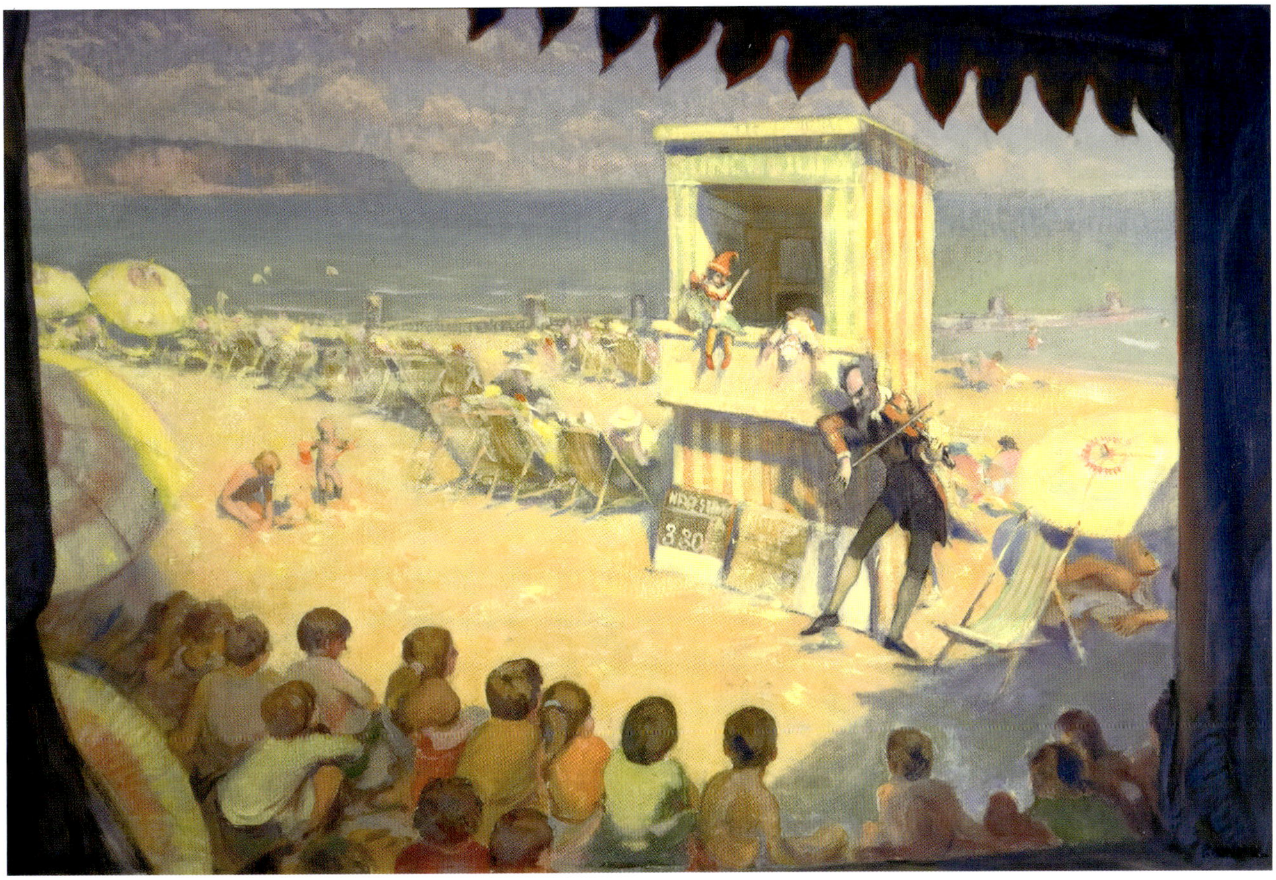

PERCIVAL WISE
Punch and Judy on Swanage Beach
1962 | oil on canvas | 595 x 895 mm
BOROUGH OF POOLE MUSEUM SERVICE

Wise exhibited *Punch and Judy on Swanage Beach* at the Russell-Cotes Art Gallery and Museum in January 1962. Eustace Nash writing in the *Bournemouth Evening Echo* commented 'What lovely colour is contained in *Punch and Judy Show* ... Bathed as it is in an atmosphere of palpitating sunlight'. Wise from his early student days at the Royal College of Art, had a feeling for beauty and especially the effects of sunlight. He has portrayed Mr Punch with a high degree of accuracy and shows him holding a stick, wearing his customary red and yellow costume with a ruff at the neck and so called 'sugar loaf' hat with tassel hanging forward in front; Judy in her mob cap and apron is slumped over the edge of the theatre, the bearded 'bottler' playing his fiddle is 'a little fanciful'.[28]

THERE IS NOTHING FANCIFUL ABOUT NANCY CARLINE'S (1909–2004) *Boats on Chesil Beach* (*c*.1990–1), which she painted in her eighties and which portrays another seaside pleasure – that of simply going out to sea in a small, open boat. Rather there is a quiet integrity and a depth of feeling to her work 'which [was] entirely true to the occasion of [its] composition. Not overly impressionist, nor expressionist, nor overly realist: her painting just brought out mysteries of light and form.'[29] It also demonstrates her keen powers of observation, a value she learnt from her painting tutor at the Slade School of Art in the late 1920s, Allan Gwynne-Jones. 'Latterly she was a frequent visitor to Portland where she painted Chesil Beach, capturing its intense luminosity' and the steep, shifting shingle bank from which boats would be launched often into ferocious seas. It was 'painted on the spot using a panel set up in her paint box. Working pictures up afterwards indoors was sometimes problematical, so she tended, especially in her later years, to work on a small scale.'[30]

28. Wendy Lalla Wharam, 20 February 2015, email correspondence to the author. Wharam had been a Punch & Judy 'Professor' on Swanage beach for eighteen seasons, in the seventies, along with Peter Jaggard. She doubted very much whether any Punch and Judy (and certainly not on Swanage beach) employed a 'bottler' like that and she had never known a fiddle player out front. Drum, panpipe accordion or concertina occasionally, but as she explained it's traditionally used as a crowd puller before the show starts.
29. Nancy Carline by her son Francis Carline and her daughter Hermione Hunter (2009): www.newenglishartclub.co.uk/pdf/friends newsletter09.pdf (accessed 12 May 2015).
30. Carline and Hunter (2009), Ibid.

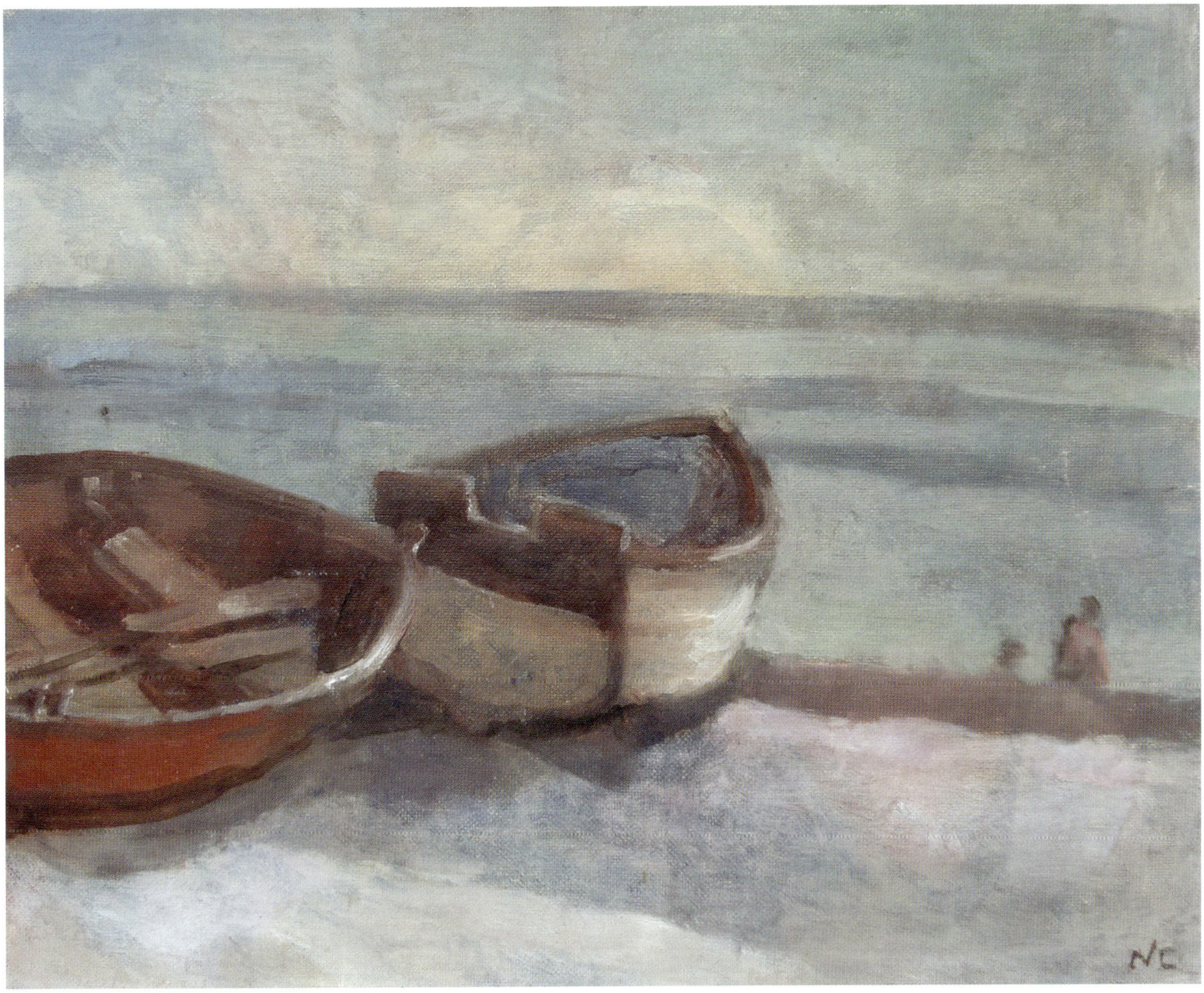

NANCY CARLINE
Boats on Chesil Beach
*c.*1990–1 | oil on canvas | 235 x 300 mm

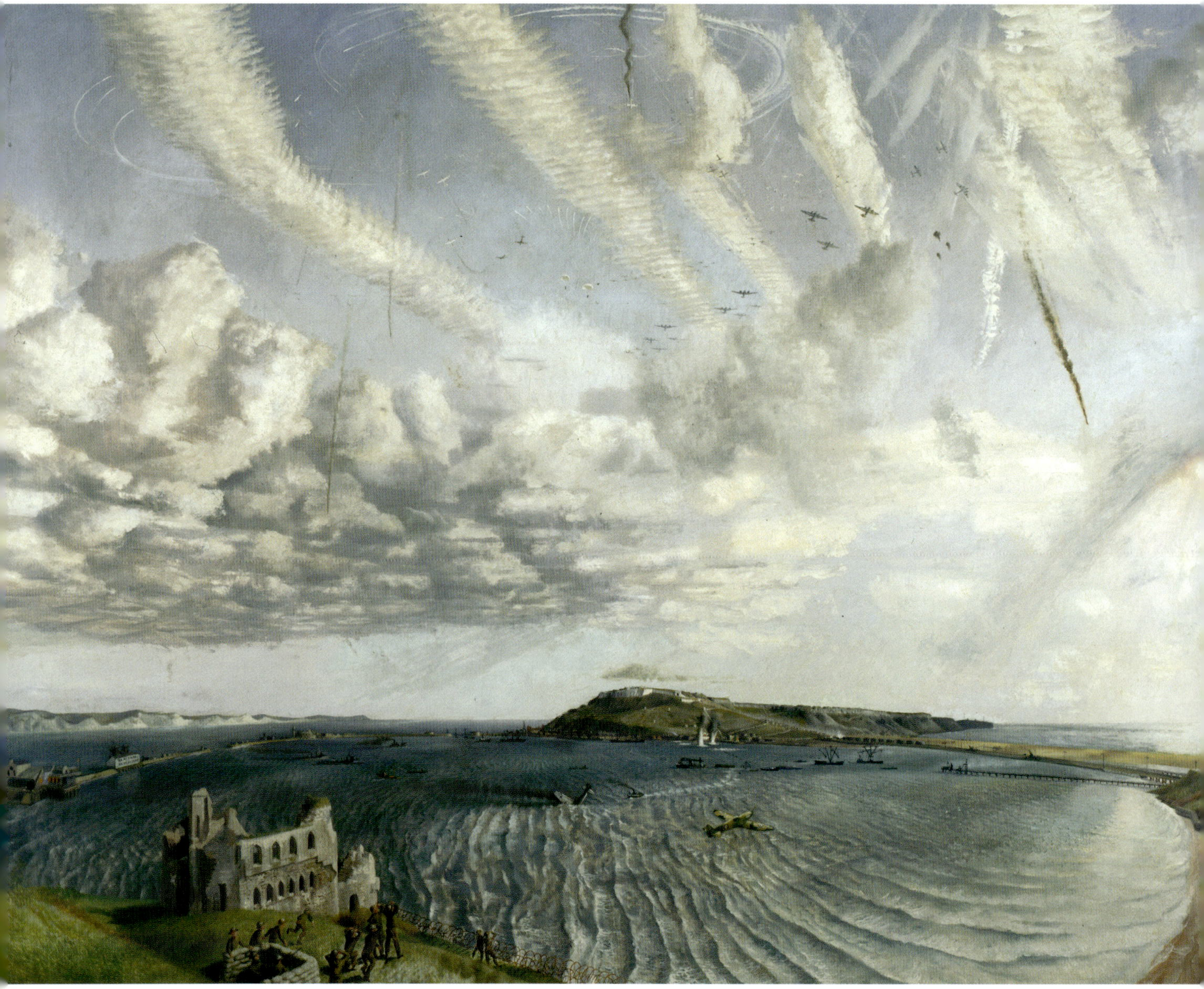

RICHARD EURICH
Air Fight over Portland
1940 | oil on canvas | 762 x 1019 mm
IMPERIAL WAR MUSEUM

RULING THE WAVES

GILL CLARKE

... This fortress built by Nature for herself
Against infection and the hand of war,
This happy breed of men, this little world,
This precious stone set in the silver sea,
Which serves it in the office of a wall,
Or as a moat defensive to a house,
Against the envy of less happier lands,
This blessed plot, this earth, this realm, this England,
... bound in with the triumphant sea
Whose rocky shore beats back the envious siege ...[1]

Although Shakespeare's silver sea with its rocky shore had both served and shielded 'this scepter'd isle' for centuries the threat of invasion across the English Channel remained. Known as The Narrow Seas to early mariners, the Channel was a mere 21½ miles wide and 216ft (58m) deep at its narrowest point and as such the south eastern coast of England was particularly vulnerable.

IN RESPONSE TO THE THREAT OF INVASION FROM EUROPE, defences along the south east and west coasts including the Solent and Cornwall were strengthened. Henry VIII ordered the construction of Hurst Castle in 1541, one of a series of 20 powerful artillery forts. Completed in 1544 with a 12-sided tower at its heart, it provided a vital defensive position protecting the entrance to the western Solent which was 'one of the two sea routes to the great commercial port of Southampton with its rich and vulnerable hinterland, to the heart of the Isle of Wight and to Portsmouth, then beginning its slow rise to prominence as a naval arsenal.'[2] The fort was refurbished and extended in response to subsequent threats during the early, mid and late nineteenth century. With the advent of the First World War in 1914 the long shingle spit leading to Hurst Castle that curves out from the Hampshire coast at Milford-on-Sea towards the Isle of Wight was closed. Searchlights were mounted in specially designed semi-circular turrets so that their beams could sweep the Needles Passage throughout the hours of darkness, and barbed wire entanglements were stretched across the beach and round the fort. In the Second World War Hurst Castle's main role was to watch for submarines and guard against surface raiders and aircraft and in July 1941 Trinity House ordered the camouflaging of the high lighthouse.

1. Shakespeare, W. (*c.*1595), *The Life and Death of Richard the Second*, Act 2, Scene 1.
2. Coad, J.G. (2004), *Hurst Castle*, English Heritage, p.15.

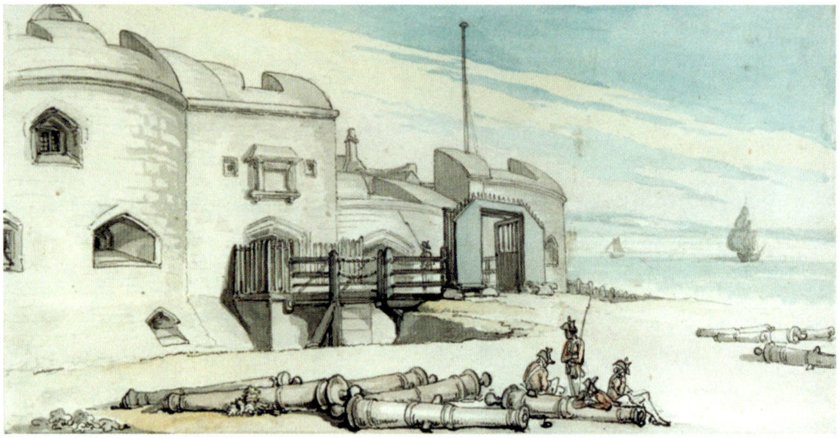

THOMAS ROWLANDSON
Hurst Castle
*c.*1790 | watercolour on paper | 124 x 235 mm

Thomas Rowlandson (1756–1827) visited the Solent coast around 1784 while on a sketching tour with his close friend the amateur artist and caricaturist Henry Wigstead (1760–1800).[3] They hired a post-chaise for their twelve-day jaunt and during this time Rowlandson was busy recording with his nimble pencil the many sights and landmarks of interest on their journey, which were later worked up to nearly seventy watercolours.[4] It is possible that whilst in the Lymington area they met the Reverend William Gilpin (1724–1804), 'champion of the Picturesque, [who] had retired as head-master of Cheam School to become vicar of the parish of Boldre in 1777.'[5]

Rowlandson was a talented and versatile artist, well known for his caricatures and draughtsmanship. This series of drawings from his tour provides important insights into his early style and technique. For up until 1780 he 'had restricted himself to penwork, in one or two drawings adding grey wash to reinforce the shadows; now he began to use watercolour to supplement the wash, what the eighteenth century called a tinted drawing, at the same time developing his subject into a more elaborate kind of narrative, replete with interrelated incident, and combining caricature with an elegant figure style.'[6]

Rowlandson returned to the area for a subsequent tour in the mid to late 1790s. One masterly result from the series was the watercolour of the west front of *Hurst Castle* complete with moat and drawbridge and captured French cannons lying on the beach with a small group of soldiers from the garrison resting on them. The plaque above the entrance records the construction of the fort and would once have held the coat of arms of Henry VIII, either side of which are the portholes through which ran the ropes or chains to lower and lift the drawbridge.[7] While sketching on the spit Rowlandson would also no doubt have encountered the local fishermen who dried their herring catches in timber sheds on the shingle.

NAPOLEON BONAPARTE (1761–1829), EMPEROR OF FRANCE FROM 1804, said of the English Channel on 16 November 1803 'It is a ditch that

3. See Christie's catalogue *Pictures and Watercolours from Longleat*, 14 June 2002, re Rowlandson and his tours.
4. See Payne, M. & Payne, J. (2010), *Regarding Thomas Rowlandson: 1757–1827: His Life, Art and Acquaintance*, Paul Holberton.
5. Payne, M. & Payne, J. (2003), 'Henry Wigstead, Rowlandson's fellow-traveller', *The British Art Journal*, vol. 4, no. 3, Autumn, p.36.
6. Hayes, J. (2008), Thomas Rowlandson, *Oxford Dictionary of National Biography*.
7. James, J. (2007), *The New Forest: A Celebration in Art*, Lymington: St Barbe Museum & Art Gallery, p.8.

shall be leaped when one is daring enough to try'. To prevent that 'leap' and to repel any invasion fleet from across the Channel 103 Martello Towers were built along the south coast during the Napoleonic Wars (1803–15). These were built largely under the direction of Brigadier-General William Twiss (1745–1827) and Captain W.H. Ford between 1805–12 in strategic locations so as to guard possible landing points. Twiss had in 1771 been engaged on the defences of Portsmouth Dockyard.

The south coast towers were a visible reminder of the threat of invasion from the French and the importance of controlling the sea for the continued security and prosperity of this island nation. The towers were numbered for identification purposes from east to west, 'starting with no. 1 above East Wear Bay to the east of Folkestone and ending with no. 73 near Beachy Head at Eastbourne, a Martello better known as the Wish Tower.'[8] It was to East Wear Bay that Adrian Hill (1895–1977) came in 1940 to undertake his recording of *Martello Tower, Folkestone, Kent* on the cliff edge directly above Copt Point with its commanding view of Folkestone Harbour to the right. The tower (numbered no. 3); was built in 1806 and also featured prominently in a painting by Turner of Folkestone in 1830. Like other towers during the Second World War it had returned to military service as an observation post and firing platform for anti-aircraft artillery.

Adrian Hill had been commissioned in the First World War following his service with the Honourable Artillery Company where as a Private in the Scouting and Sniping Section his artistic skills had been put to good use sketching the position of the enemy. He was the first (and youngest) artist to be commissioned by the Imperial War Museum on 27 December 1917 to document aspects of the war; this followed his being invalided home after being badly gassed.[9] He returned to France where he produced nearly two hundred vivid pen and wash drawings on the spot of water-logged trenches, derelict tanks, ruined churches and devastated villages. Hill was well used to drawing in odd positions and environments and Folkestone was no exception; indeed as the Second World War progressed coastal areas became more strictly controlled and permits needed before records could be made. He was one of 97 artists, men and women, 63 of whom were like him specially commissioned to 'make a number of topographical watercolour drawings of places and buildings of characteristic national interest, particularly those exposed to the danger of destruction by the operations of war.'[10]

The scheme, which was established in the winter of 1939–40 and intended to boost national morale ran until 1943, reaffirmed what Britain was fighting for. Funded by the Pilgrim Trust, it came to be called 'Recording the changing face of Britain' and over 1500 works were eventually produced by some of the country's finest watercolour painters including Stanley Badmin, Sir William Russell Flint, Thomas Hennell, Charles Knight, John Piper and Kenneth Rowntree. It was the brainchild of Sir Kenneth Clark, Director of the National Gallery and chairman of the War Artists' Advisory Committee (WAAC), who saw the two schemes operating in tandem. Recording Britain as noted focussed largely on rural buildings and the countryside whereas the War Artists' scheme charged artists with making an artistic record of war in all its aspects for posterity, be they 'facts, drama, human emotions and life generally.'[11] This included reporting on the two main facets of civilian effort,

8. James, J. (2007), *The New Forest: A Celebration in Art*, Lymington: St Barbe Museum & Art Gallery, p.63.
9. See Gough, P. (2010), *A Terrible Beauty: British Artists in the First World War*, Sansom & Co., and Harries, M. and S. (1983), *The War Artists. British Official War Art of the Twentieth Century*, Michael Joseph in Association with The Imperial War Museum & The Tate Gallery.
10. Macmillan, Chairman of the Pilgrim Trust (1946), 'Introduction', *Recording Britain*, 1, Oxford University Press in association with the Pilgrim Trust, p.v.
11. Clark, K. (1942), 'War Artists at the National Gallery', *The Studio*, vol. 123, no. 586, January, p.2.

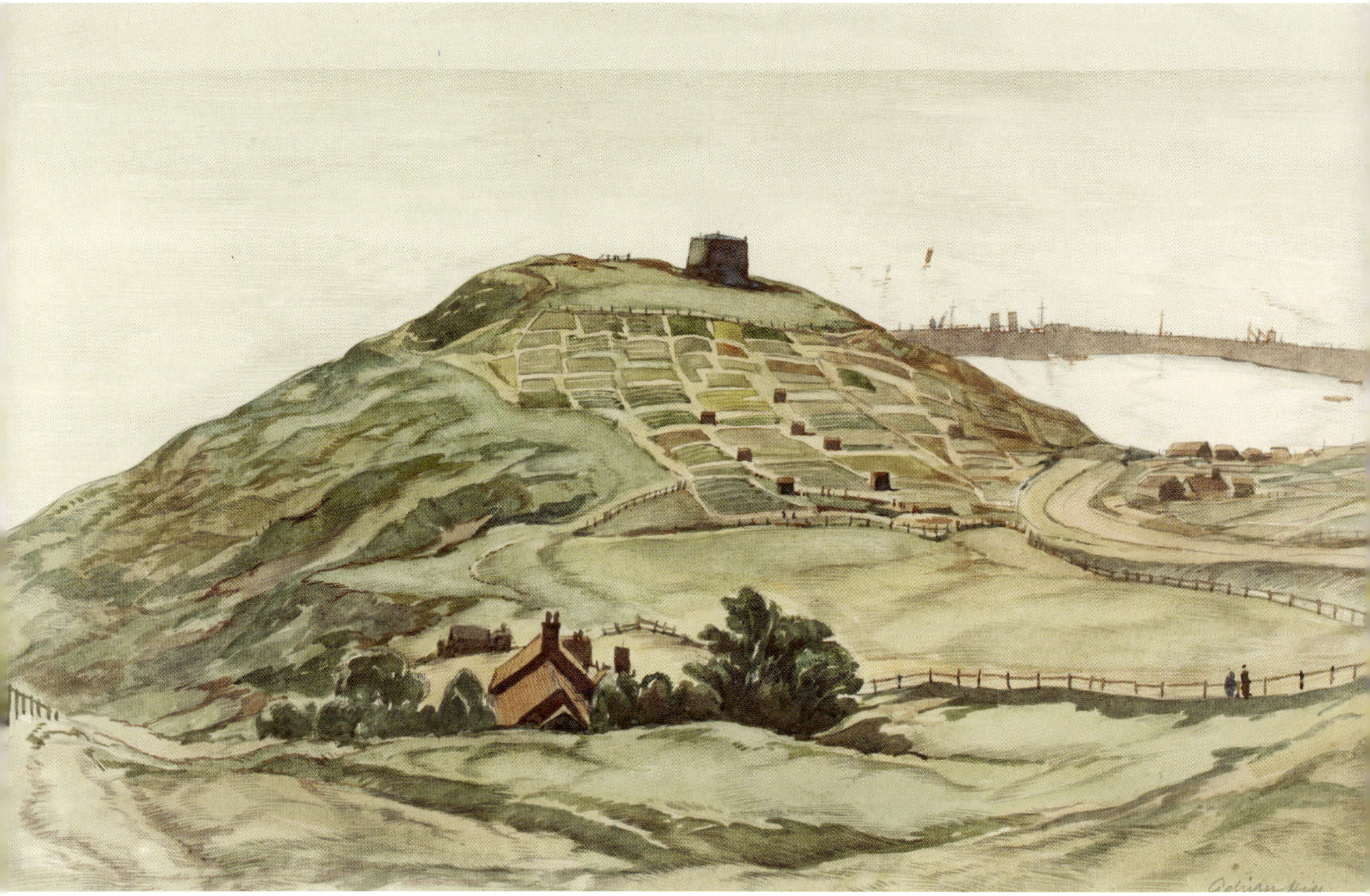

ADRIAN HILL
Martello Tower, Folkestone, Kent
*c.*1940 | watercolour | 314 x 489 mm
VICTORIA AND ALBERT MUSEUM. GIVEN BY THE PILGRIM TRUST

namely work on the land and the production of armaments. The scheme was also designed 'to show contemporaries at home and overseas something of our war effort.'[12]

The small, squat Martello Tower recorded by Hill with its walls up to 13 feet thick towards the sea and 5 feet to landward is 'silhouetted against a calm sea, [and] is the central focus of a wider view which encompasses ... a patchwork of allotments laid out on the leeward side of the promontory ... From Hill's vantage point the town itself is invisible, tucked away below the cliffs – his subject is rather the nation's strategies of defence against invasion, past and present. The allotments, product of the patriotic drive towards self-sufficiency symbolise the spirit of the home front. The Martello stands for the continuity of independence and a history of resistance to European domination.'[13]

THAT HISTORY OF RESISTANCE WAS MUCH IN EVIDENCE IN Portsmouth, indeed, the essayist and political pamphleteer Daniel Defoe (*c.*1660–1731) on his arrival in the port in 1722 on a tour through 'the Whole Island of Great Britain' found it 'the largest fortification, beyond comparison; that we have in England', chosen 'for the best security to the navy above all places in Britain; the entrance into the harbour is safe, but very narrow, guarded on both sides by terrible platforms of canon ...'.[14] Such security meant that by the mid-eighteenth century the Royal Navy Dockyard (Portsmouth was one of six) was the prime base for victualling and repairs to the fleet. By the advent of the Napoleonic Wars 15,000 men were employed in the Royal Navy Dockyards, and of these some 3,900 were employed in Portsmouth, which was at this time the world's largest industrial complex.[15]

The marine artist George Chambers (1803–40) was well qualified to paint *Entrance to Portsmouth Harbour* in the 1830s having gone to sea at the age of ten in the Humber-keel *Experiment*, his uncle being both owner and captain. Two years later he was apprenticed on the brig *Equity* and it was here that his talent and delight in painting began to develop. His biographer, and somewhat partisan admirer, the poet and chartist John Watkins (1808–58) whom he first met in 1832 described how he seldom went ashore when in harbour, except on a Sunday to church, to see the pictures in it. Chambers' small stature meant that he was often ill-treated and his size rendered him unequal to heavy tasks, such that he was chiefly employed in jobs of painting. After some five years he was enabled to cancel his indenture and return to his home town of Whitby before going by ship to London around 1823 to further his career as an artist securing the patronage of admirals and royalty. Having been a mariner Chambers was able to employ in his paintings not only 'Mechanical exactness in the rigging, shape, and trim of vessels [that] can only be learnt from practical observation'[16] but also great fidelity in his depth of colouring and representation of water. Attributes that were praised by fellow artists including Turner and Constable.

Chambers always carried a small sketchbook and would on occasions take a boat to sketch choice bits in the harbour. He painted in his drawing-room where he would first 'chalk in the subject, then pencil it, washing out the chalk marks. He first rubbed in the sky, afterwards the more prominent parts of the picture, but not piece by piece – he generally had the whole of the picture

12. Anon. (1944), *War Pictures at the National Gallery*, p.1.
13. Mellor, D., Saunders, G. & Wright, P. (1990), *Recording Britain. A Pictorial Doomsday of Pre-War Britain*, David & Charles in association with the V&A Museum, p.92.
14. Bardell, M. (2012), *The Isle of Wight, Portsmouth & the Solent: A Cultural History*, Signal Books, p.88.
15. See Brown, P. (2005), *Maritime Portsmouth: A History and Guide*, Tempus, p.21.
16. Watkins, J. (1841), *Life and Career of George Chambers*, London: Printed for the Author and sold by him at no. 9, Bell Yard, Fleet St., p.60.

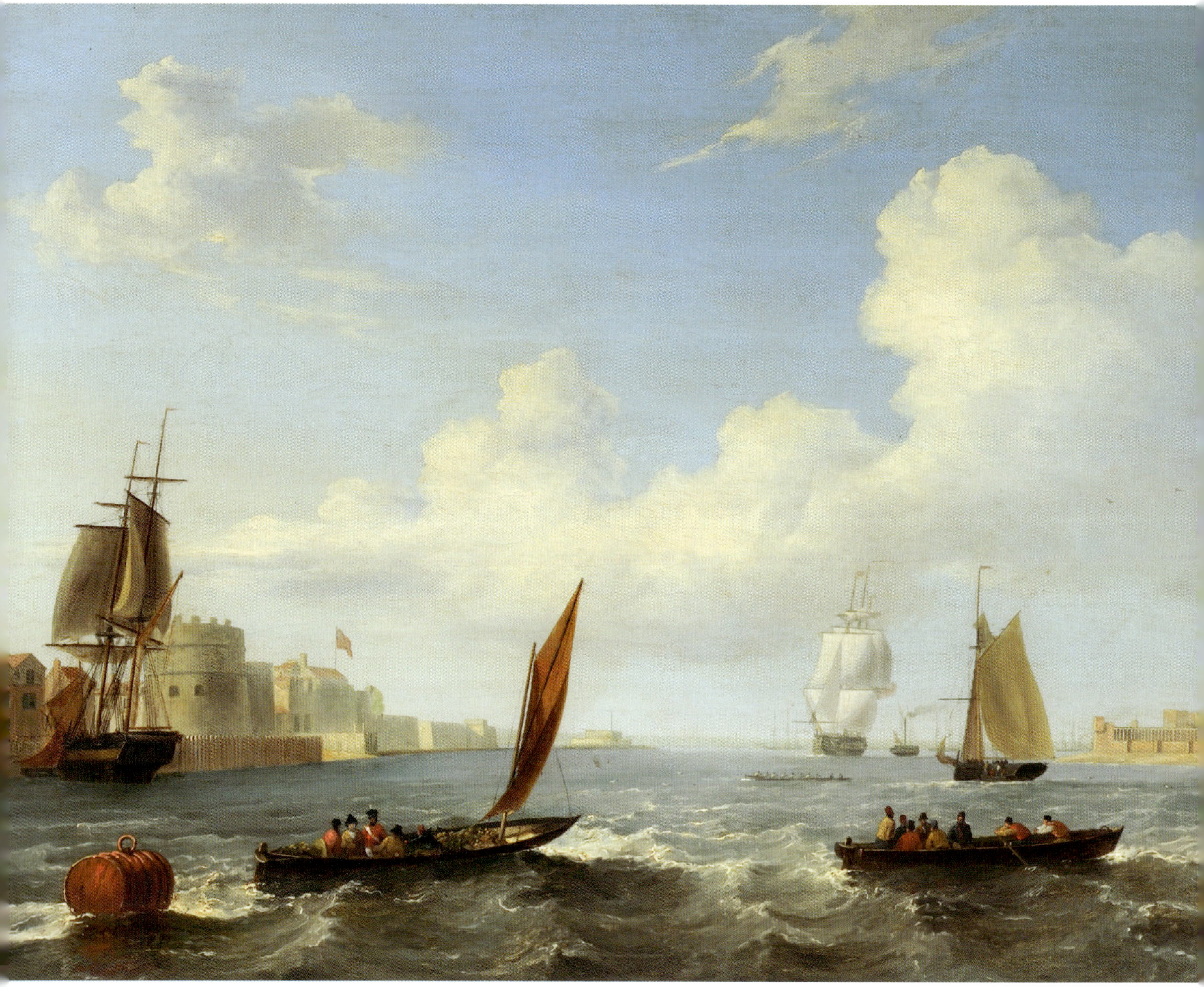

GEORGE CHAMBERS
Entrance to Portsmouth Harbour
oil on canvas | 439 x 596 mm
REPRODUCED BY KIND PERMISSION OF PORTSMOUTH MUSEUM SERVICE, PORTSMOUTH CITY COUNCIL

equally advanced, for he could not finish bit by bit. His method when at work was to paint a few strokes, then retire to see how they looked, return and rub them out with a cloth, or put in others, retire again and so on until he produced the effect which he saw in his 'mind's eye'. Sometimes he used his fingers and sometimes the stick end of his brush.'[17]

Portsmouth harbour entrance was a popular subject for artists and one that Chambers returned to with some success. His detailed and faithful composition includes a number of large vessels together with the powerful fortifications built (and modified) over the preceding centuries on the south west facing shore. These included the Round Tower, on the small peninsula known as The Point, which commenced about 1418. The Square Tower, which was begun in 1494 and Southsea Castle which was another of the series of forts constructed for Henry VIII in some haste in 1544; its position rendering it key to guarding the harbour entrance. On the Gosport side can be glimpsed Fort Blockhouse, and perhaps *en route* to the Fort are the two small wherry boats manned by watermen who have just rounded the large buoy in order to transport their passengers, including sailors from their ships and goods across the harbour.

Around the time of Chambers' death in 1840 Portsmouth Dockyard witnessed a period of expansion largely thanks to the development of steam vessels. Lord Palmerston speaking in the House of Commons on 30 July 1845 said 'The Channel is no longer a barrier. Steam navigation has rendered that which was before impassable by a military force nothing more than a river passable by a steam bridge.'[18] The period of peace that had followed the Battle of Waterloo in 1815 was no longer assured with the knowledge that France according to Palmerston had steamers that could transport 30,000 men across the silver sea. In response to these invasion fears new longer docks and building slips were built to enable the installation of steam machinery together with further coastal fortifications. The general assumption was that Britannia still ruled the waves but the turn of the twentieth century witnessed the rise of new enemies and new threats to diplomatic and defence policy. In 1906 HMS *Dreadnought*, the most advanced battleship in the world and the first to be powered by steam turbines, was launched in Portsmouth. The race for naval supremacy was now with Germany.

THE FIRST WORLD WAR

THE FIRST WORLD WAR HERALDED A SHIFT IN THE FOCUS OF Portsmouth Dockyard away from the construction of battleships to the refit and repair of over 1,600 ships during the years 1914–18 and this was accompanied by the employment of women in every workshop. It was to the busy Dockyard that the Scottish Colourist John Duncan Fergusson (1874–1961) travelled in late July 1918 where his attention was drawn to 'The shapes of the submarines and destroyers moored at the quayside, [and which he] painted with an awareness of the Vorticist work of Wyndham Lewis and William Roberts, [which] took the place of the dancers and portraits on which he had concentrated since returning to Britain'[19] when the war had forced him reluctantly to return from France where he had mingled with the likes of Matisse and Picasso in Paris.

17. Watkins, J. (1841), *Life and Career of George Chambers*, London: Printed for the Author and sold by him at no. 9, Bell Yard, Fleet St., p.85.
18. Palmerston (1845), cited in Longmate, N. (2001), *Island Fortress: The Defence of Great Britain 1603–1945*, Pimlico, p.308.
19. Billcliffe, R. (undated), 'John Duncan Fergusson (1874–1961): Life and Work', in *The Fergusson Gallery Guidebook*, p.10.

Fergusson was called up when the upper age limit for enlistment was raised to 41 in the spring of 1918 having previously done all he could to avoid active service in France. He and his partner Margaret Morris (1891–1980) the dance pioneer, choreographer and teacher saw the war as something of an inconvenience.

Fergusson's medical was arranged for 6 June, he duly passed being graded A.1. After some petitioning to the Admiralty he was exempted and granted a six-week commission by the British War Memorials Committee (BWMC) to paint dockyard scenes in Portsmouth. Fergusson had sailed boats all his life and in a letter to Alfred Yockney, Secretary of the BWMC written after his stay in Portsmouth he revealed that he had found inspiration there that he had not had before in his work. Never an official war artist Fergusson was mightily relieved that his Navy uniform was to be blue, his favourite colour, as he disliked the khaki colour of Army uniforms. He was however much annoyed that until its arrival he 'was frequently hindered by over-zealous workmen reporting him to the police for spying.'[20] He wrote to Morris in London on 30 July having visited Southsea and found it very like the south of France and informed her that the George Hotel was quite good and the food excellent and that he had been round the docks with the Commander in a boat. Fergusson said 'it was very fine to paint, but takes a bit of time to select ...'.[21] Three days later his anxiety was over as he had selected 'several splendid things', although there remained some formalities to be concluded. Morris visited him in Portsmouth and found him in great form. The result of his sojourn was a large number of 'conté and pastel drawings, which were later transformed into a series of distinctive studio based paintings. In these his tendencies towards a new language of simplified geometric shapes portrayed within shallow space evolved.'[22]

Dockyard, Portsmouth 'is no moral comment on the war,'[23] indeed, the Dazzle-camouflaged and alarmingly tilting bows of the destroyer awaiting repair gives the harbour something of a Mediterranean feel with its contrasting bold, abstract stripes of blue, red, black, grey and white. The large metal wheel of a dockside crane, dominates the foreground to the left, although it looks more like a wheel at a fairground, beneath it is a circular red lever and an empty burnished metal cylinder. A small green dinghy nestles beside the destroyer with two figures in it perhaps about to effect much needed repairs. The far dockside is lined with dock wagons, and what appears to be Dazzle-camouflaged ships and buildings beyond.

Dazzle camouflage transformed the look not only of vessels but also of dockyards during the First World War. Its inventor in 1917, the artist Lieutenant-Commander Norman Wilkinson RNVR (Royal Naval Volunteer Reserve) saw it as a way of responding to the threat posed to British shipping by torpedoes from German submarines. His paper 'The Dazzle Painting of Ships' published in the *Journal of the Royal Society of Arts* in March 1920 sought to explain the reasons for its adoption and how he spoke with some experience having been a marine painter with long experience at sea where he had constantly observed the weather, colour and like.

Wilkinson realised that it was impossible to paint a ship to achieve invisibility but if it were painted in such a way that all accepted forms of the ship were broken up by masses of strongly contrasted colour, it would

20. Surry, N. (2008), *A Portsmouth Canvas: The Art of the City and the Sea 1770–1970*, The Fortune Press, p.58.
21. Morris, M. (1974, reprinted 2010), *The Art of J.D. Fergusson: A Biased Biography by Margaret Morris*, Blackie, p.123.
22. Simister, K. (2001), *Living Paint: J.D. Fergusson 1874–1961*, Mainstream Publishing, p.75.
23. Strang, A. (2015), 'A Scottish Colourist's Great War: J.D. Fergusson's Work for the Admiralty', paper presented at the *Scottish Society for Art History, Study Day*, Perth.

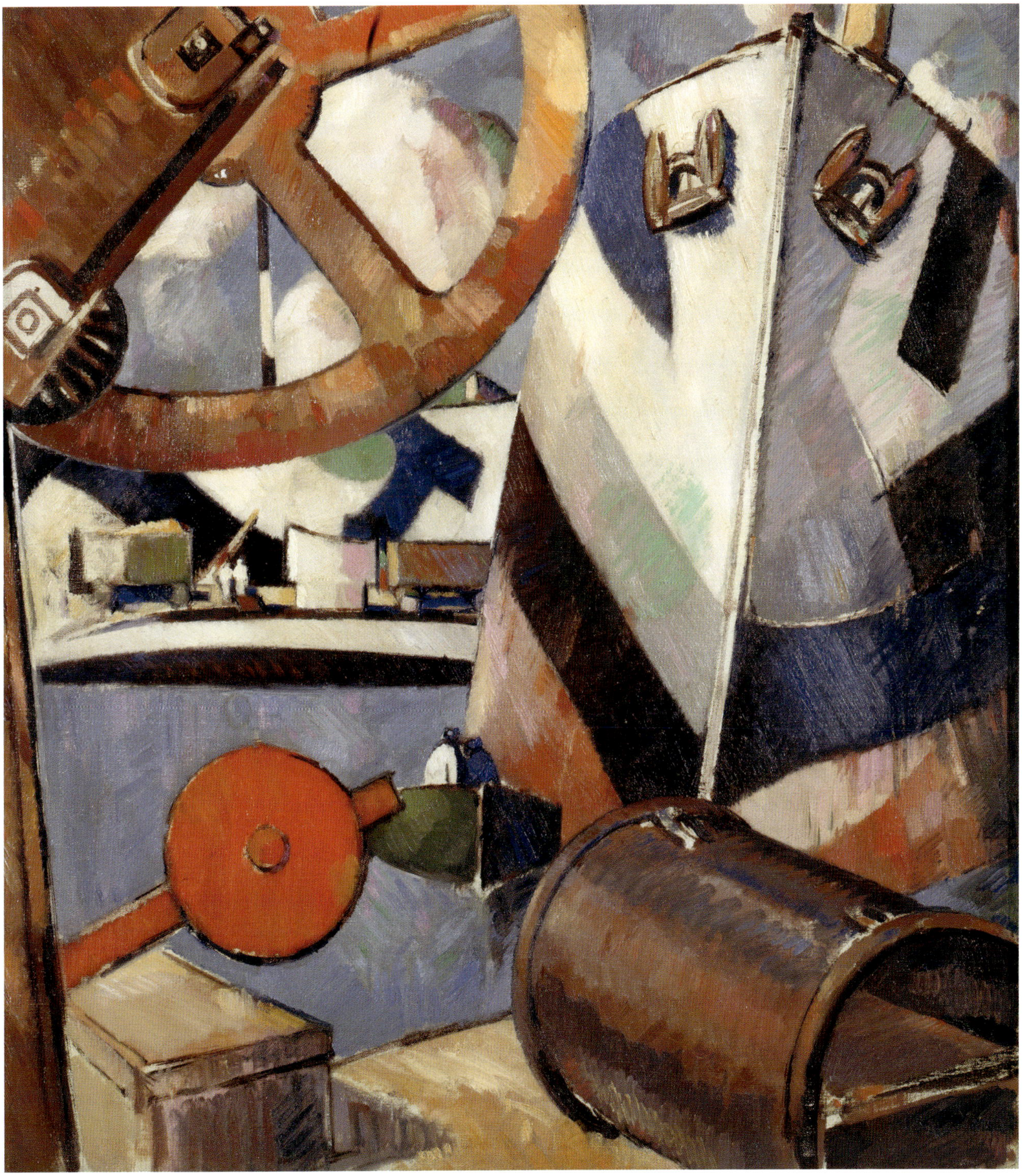

J.D. FERGUSSON
Dockyard, Portsmouth
1918 | oil on canvas | 770 x 688 mm
IMPERIAL WAR MUSEUM, IMAGE COURTESY OF THE FERGUSSON GALLERY, PERTH & KINROSS COUNCIL

make it a matter of some difficulty for a submarine to decide on the exact course of the vessel to be attacked. Following approval by the Admiralty all merchant vessels and armed merchant ships together with certain of HM ships (convoying cruisers, destroyers, minelayers and those working with merchant vessels) were Dazzle-painted; sloping lines, curves and stripes were found to give the greatest distortion. Designs were as varied as possible and always different on both sides of a ship so as to maximise the element of surprise. The leading Vorticist and print maker Edward Wadsworth (1889–1949) was also employed to develop Dazzle camouflage and in this role oversaw its application to ships in Liverpool Docks in July 1918. More than 2,300 British ship were Dazzle-painted during the war.

CHRISTOPHER RICHARD WYNNE NEVINSON (1889–1946) UNLIKE Fergusson produced some of the most chilling and bleak images of the war as a result of his direct experience of the horror and brutality of the conflict in France and Flanders having served as a Red Cross orderly and later with the Royal Army Medical Corps before rheumatic fever led to his discharge in 1916. Nevinson applied to be a war artist in April 1917 and returned to France where he witnessed the preparations for the Passchendaele campaign, returning in early August. Over the next seven months he produced over 70 paintings and prints related to the war. While *Loading Timber at Southampton Docks* which was completed later in 1917 could scarcely be called chilling, it is nonetheless striking with its largely dark colours and bold simplifications it has echoes of Nevinson's early Cubist/Futurist work. It evinces something sinister and menacing about the crowded dockside with its cranes, transatlantic steamers and ant-like workers walking up the gang planks with timber on their shoulders while the heavier timber is winched up by crane.

Timber was a vital commodity and the fact that Nevinson was detailed to record it is testament to that importance. Southampton Docks became a closed port and only vessels working under the Admiralty could enter it. Known officially as No.1 Military Port it was vital to the transport of goods during the war and it acted as the main port for military embarkation. Over eight million troops passed through Southampton on their way to the Western Front where they would have much need for timber given the endless mud and great water-filled craters, and pressure to maintain lines of communication and supplies. The Timber Cutting Section of The Women's Land Army, and later The Women's Forestry Service, played a crucial part in Britain, felling trees, measuring and sawing timber into lengths, and stacking and carting the results of their labours to be transported to the docks. A recruiting leaflet pointed out the need for members to provide timber for the Navy and the Army, stating 'Our Sailors need Wood for their Ships. Our Soldiers need Wood for their Railways, their Shelters and their Aeroplanes.'[24]

Over the course of the First World War some 30 artists recorded maritime events and personnel and in so doing 'every Branch of the British Navy with regard to types of ships, bases and areas involved in naval operations' were represented, the artists being charged to endeavour that the results were 'worthy as sea pictures to hand down to posterity, both as regards subject and quality of art'. In the Second World War about 40 more artists, some of whom like Wilkinson had also served in the First World War were involved in recording similar events.[25]

24. See Clarke, G. (2008), *The Women's Land Army: A Portrait*, Sansom & Co.
25. See Harries, M. and S. (1983), Op. cit., p.130, and Brook-Hart, D. (1981), *Twentieth Century British Marine Painting*, Antique Collectors' Club, p.30.

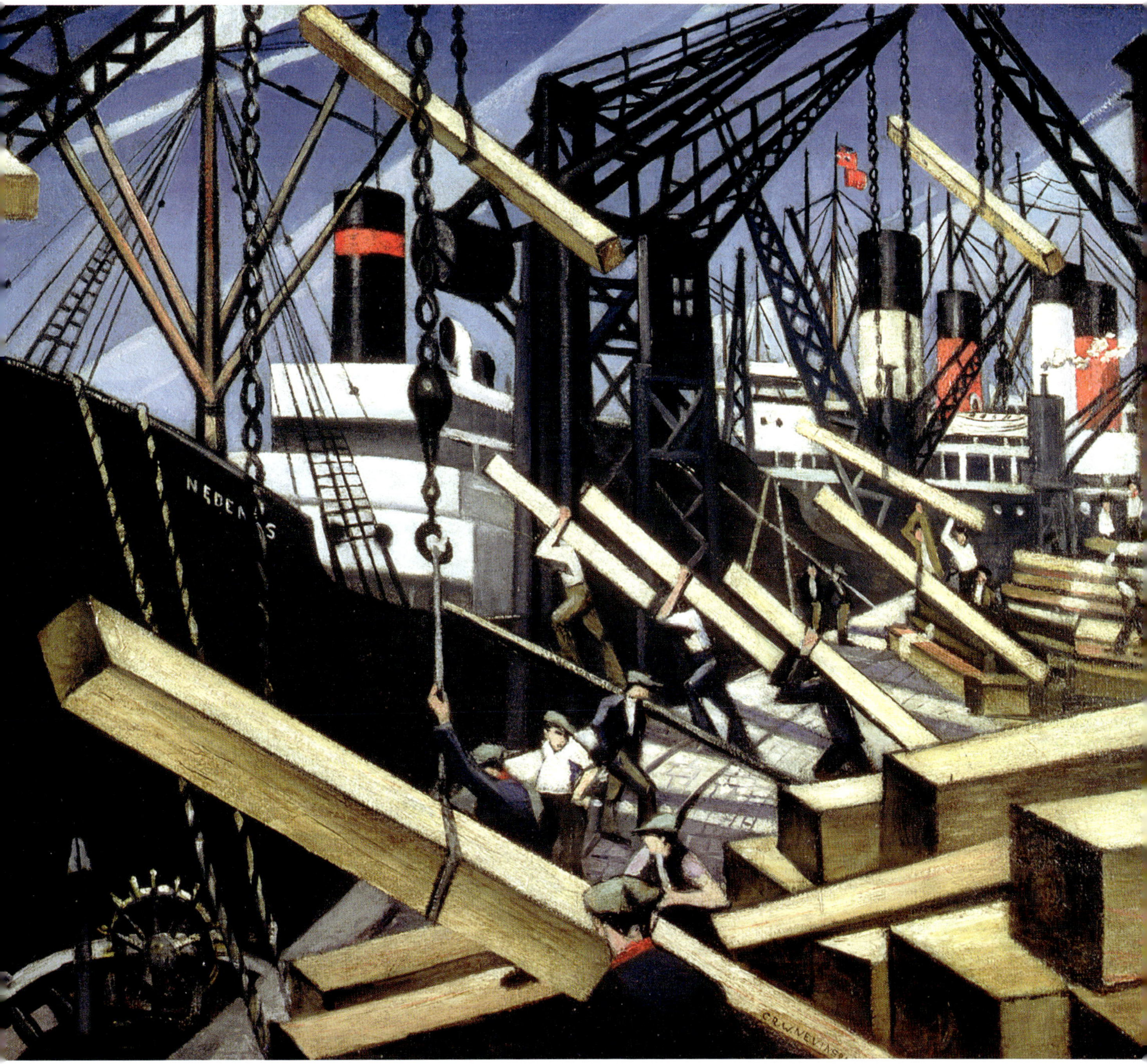

CHRISTOPHER NEVINSON
Loading Timber at Southampton Docks
1917 | oil on canvas | 510 x 610 mm
SOUTHAMPTON CITY ART GALLERY/BRIDGEMAN IMAGES

THE SECOND WORLD WAR

THE OUTBREAK OF THE SECOND WORLD WAR ON 1 SEPTEMBER 1939 endangered once again the liberty of this island nation. The following year with the threat of imminent invasion the new Prime Minister Winston Churchill went to the House of Commons on 4 June to report on the evacuation of Allied troops from the beaches of northern France and said 'We shall defend our Island, whatever the cost may be. We shall fight on the beaches, we shall fight on the landing grounds, we shall fight in the fields and in the streets, we shall fight in the hills; we shall never surrender ...'.

Some six days later the painter Richard Eurich (1903–92) who was a Quaker and pacifist and who at the outset of the war had volunteered for service as an ambulance driver and Air Raid Protection warden, was prompted by the events in Dunkirk to write to Sir Kenneth Clark, chairman of the WAAC saying 'This surely should be painted and I am wondering if I should be considered for the job! It seems to me that the traditional sea-painting of Van der Velde and Turner should be carried on to enrich our heritage.' Eurich was given the opportunity to do the job and he completed *The Withdrawal from Dunkirk* in just three weeks; it was shown at the National Gallery as part of the first 'Exhibition of Picture by War Artists' in late August 1940 to much critical acclaim. The success was in part due to the fact that 'in the summer of 1939 Eurich had made a sketching trip to Dunkirk and, with his notes and exceedingly acute memory for the detail of seascape, had an intimate working knowledge of the beaches.'[26] In November 1940 Eurich was commissioned to undertake *Air Fight over Portland* (page 78) – it was delivered to the WAAC in January 1941. The following month he was appointed as a full-time salaried Official War Artist to the Admiralty and given an honorary commission with the customary rank of Captain in the Royal Marines. He went on to produce over 30 paintings of naval subjects many of which admirably demonstrated his mastery of seascapes and the power of his visual memory.

Eurich saw his role as recording events as accurately as possible, a feat he achieved with some distinction in *Air Fight over Portland*. During its genesis he would regularly cycle over to Portland, a place he knew well, to make notes and sketches. The painting was described in some length in *War at Sea* (1942), one of a series of small booklets of *War Pictures by British Artists* published by Oxford University Press. 'The scene is Portland and the time a day in September, 1940, when over forty German aircraft were brought down in a very short action. The bombers are coming up through the thin low cloud protected by fighters only just visible above them. Our fighters have already dived through them and shot some down. The rest have scattered and are chasing. One German bomber has come down in the roads. Two German airmen are seen descending by parachutes. The white condensation trails in the sky show where the fighters have been at work.' The ruins in the foreground are Sandsfoot Castle, part of Henry VIII's coastal defences, built around 1539.

ALTHOUGH ERIC RAVILIOUS (1903–42) WAS THE SAME AGE AS Eurich and both were appointed to the Admiralty they had little else in common, indeed Ravilious 'became involved with the sea as a subject

26. Harries, M. and S. (1983), Op. cit., p.219.

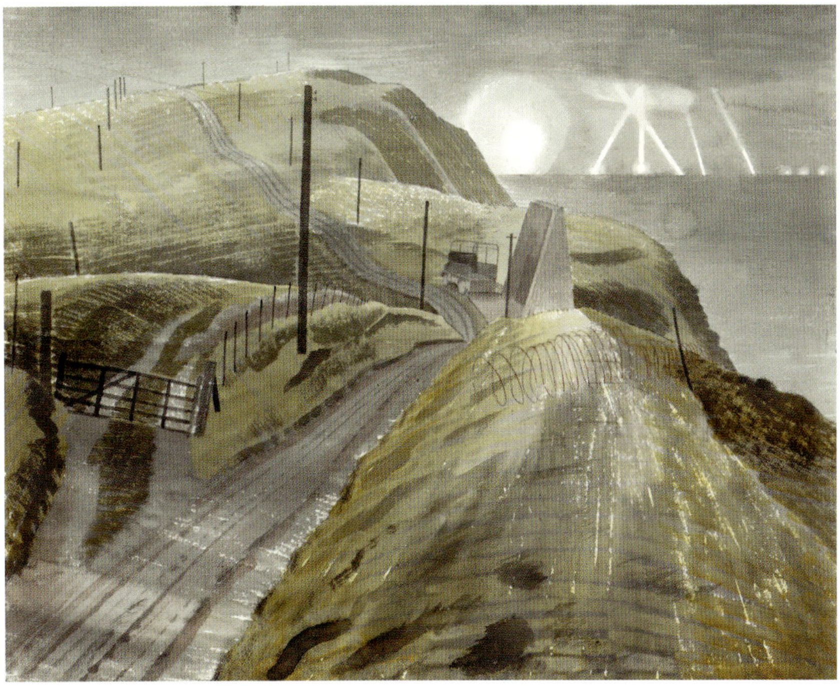

ERIC RAVILIOUS
Bombing the Channel Ports
1941 | watercolour on paper | 387 x 488 mm
IMPERIAL WAR MUSEUM

largely through the accident of war.'[27] Initially Ravilious served with the Observer Corps at Castle Hedingham, but on 24 December 1939 he received a letter from Reginald Gleadowe, the Admiralty representative on the WAAC informing him that he and John Nash (1893–1977) had been selected to work on a part-time basis. The following day he wrote to his father-in-law, Colonel F.S. Garwood expressing his excitement while at the same time acknowledging that it would be 'odd to join the Navy and see the World after being tethered to my Observation post for so long.'[28] The six-month contract began on 10 February 1940, John Nash who had been an official artist in the First World War, covered the Western approaches while Ravilious's early commissions took him to Chatham, Sheerness, Whitstable, Grimsby, Norway and the Arctic Circle. In the summer of 1940 he went to *HMS Dolphin* at Gosport where he made lithographs of submarine interiors before he embarked on a series of depictions of coastal defences between Newhaven and Dover.

Bombing the Channel Ports (1941) with its soft colours shows the ghostly white beams of the searchlights in the distance probing the sky to identify bombers for anti-aircraft guns to target. The landscape is littered with the paraphernalia of war and midway along the deserted coastal path between Folkestone and Dover Ravilious's fascination and interest in machinery is evidenced by his depiction of The Abbot's Cliff sound (or acoustic) mirror (a forerunner of radar) on the edge of the chalky cliff top above East Wear Bay. A spectacular remnant of a series of large concrete concave disks some 20 feet in diameter built between 1914–34 to capture the sound of incoming enemy aircraft and provide an early warning as they flew over the North Sea and Channel towards England, it stands obsolete, mute-like, facing rows of telegraph poles spaced out regimentally across the grey-green hills as they

27. Ross, A. (1983), *Colours of War: War Art 1939–45*, Jonathan Cape, p.95.
28. See letter no. 23 in *Ravilious at War* edited by Anne Ullmann (2002), and published by The Fleece Press, p.41.

disappear over the horizon. 'The painting lacks a fine finish, which suggests that more work was intended. If so, it is no disadvantage. The broader work with colours merged while wet, working against highlights saved with a resist applied before the washes, shows a more painterly side of Ravilious with less caution and care for detail. It is impossible to know how much work he did on the site, in this case in the dark, and how much was reconstructed from memory, but the paint here seems to suggest immediacy.'[29]

COASTAL SUBJECTS WERE ALSO PAINTED BY JOHN PLATT (1886–1967) a Ministry of War Transport artist from the spring of 1943–4. A successful woodcut artist and stained glass designer he had served in the Royal Army Service Corps (Transport) in the First World War. Working from his studio in Putney he documented wartime traffic on the River Thames but owing to his slowness in completing work his commission was not renewed. Fortunately *Convoy Arriving off St. Anthony's Lighthouse, Falmouth* was completed prior to this in 1942. Admiral Sir Herbert Richmond (1871–1946) in his Introduction to *War at Sea* (1942) pointed to the important and changing role of the war artist and the challenges that it brings insofar as 'The whole nature of the sea battle has in fact changed, and in this war there are no great fleets composed of mass bodies of ships of the line ... Nor are the British battleships all concentrated, as they were in the last war, in one great mass ... Convoys are assembling and sailing ... The merchant ship, sailing sometimes in convoy, sometimes alone and trusting to its speed and its own armaments, is carrying our goods.' Convoys had been reintroduced in the First World War and proved an effective counter-measure to submarine attacks and were an important means of transporting the Army and keeping the nation fed and supplied; food was seen as a munition of war. Command of the sea (and indeed of the air) was crucial.

The merchant ships in the convoy depicted by Platt have had the good fortune to have a well-armed naval escort, probably a Hunt Type 1-class escort destroyer, to prevent them from being easy targets for U-boat attack. In addition they are flying kite balloons to discourage enemy dive bombers as they approach Falmouth. Saint Anthony's Lighthouse, situated at the eastern side of the entrance to Falmouth Harbour, was built by Trinity House in 1835; painted in camouflage, it warns ships of the dangers of Black Rock in the centre of the channel into the harbour and of the Manacles, south of the harbour entrance. In the background to right and left is the harbour of Falmouth with shipping and Pendennis Castle built between 1539–45 on the headland to the left, above the town. A large bell, serving as a fog signal, hangs from the tower of the lighthouse, which flies the Trinity House flag. Two signallers have been positioned on the balcony and on the right an army patrol prepares to descend the steps towards the lighthouse.[30]

CONVOYS WERE RECORDED BY A NUMBER OF ARTISTS INCLUDing Eurich who produced *Attack on a Convoy Seen From the Air* (1941) in which the Needles can be glimpsed through the clouds, off the western tip of the Isle of Wight and by John Nash who contributed *Convoy Scene*. Norman Wilkinson (1878–1971) was one of the first eight artists to be commissioned

29. Powers, A. (2013), *Eric Ravilious Artist & Designer*, Lund Humphries, p.169 and p.171.
30. See Royal Museums Greenwich – National Maritime Museum: http://collections.rmg.co.uk/collections/objects/13152.html (accessed 19 April 2015).

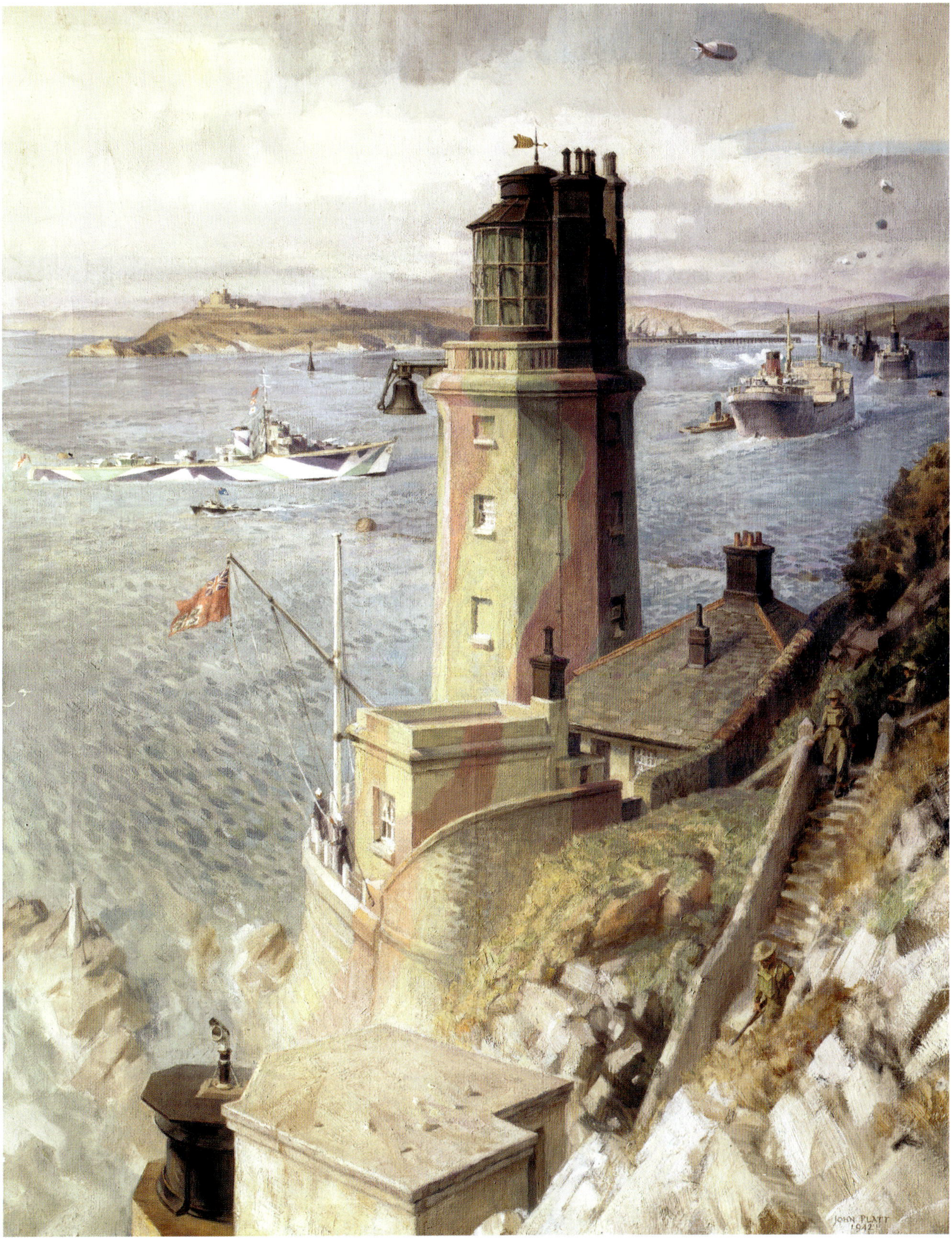

JOHN PLATT
Convoy Arriving off St. Anthony's Lighthouse, Falmouth
1942 | oil on canvas | 913 x 710 mm

in the First World War and recorded the Gallipoli engagements on the spot; he completed *Beachy Head: Attack on Convoy* (*c*.1942–4) just after he had resigned from the Air Ministry where as Honorary Air Commodore he had been employed as Inspector of Camouflage, under the Directorate of Works. This painting forms part of his series, 'The War at Sea' in which he travelled extensively to document the work of both the Royal and Merchant Navy and Coastal Command.

Beachy Head: Attack on Convoy shows the RAF defending a convoy under enemy fighter-bomber attack near a particularly vulnerable part of the Sussex coast. An aircraft crashes into the sea close to the promontory of Beachy Head, followed by a trail of smoke, in the distance are pilots descending in their parachutes from shot-down planes. The lighthouse stands defiant. Wilkinson's assured handling of colour and his understanding of the sea is in the vein of the Old Master sea painters and results in a composition imbued both with violence and likely death juxtaposed against gleaming chalky cliffs and shimmering sea, reminiscent of the travel posters he designed in the early 1900s. As the English dramatist and writer Douglas Jerrold (1803–57) pithily said, the liberty of England was preserved in brine – the brine being the British Channel. The effects of two World Wars testify to the value of the so-called 'silver streak'.

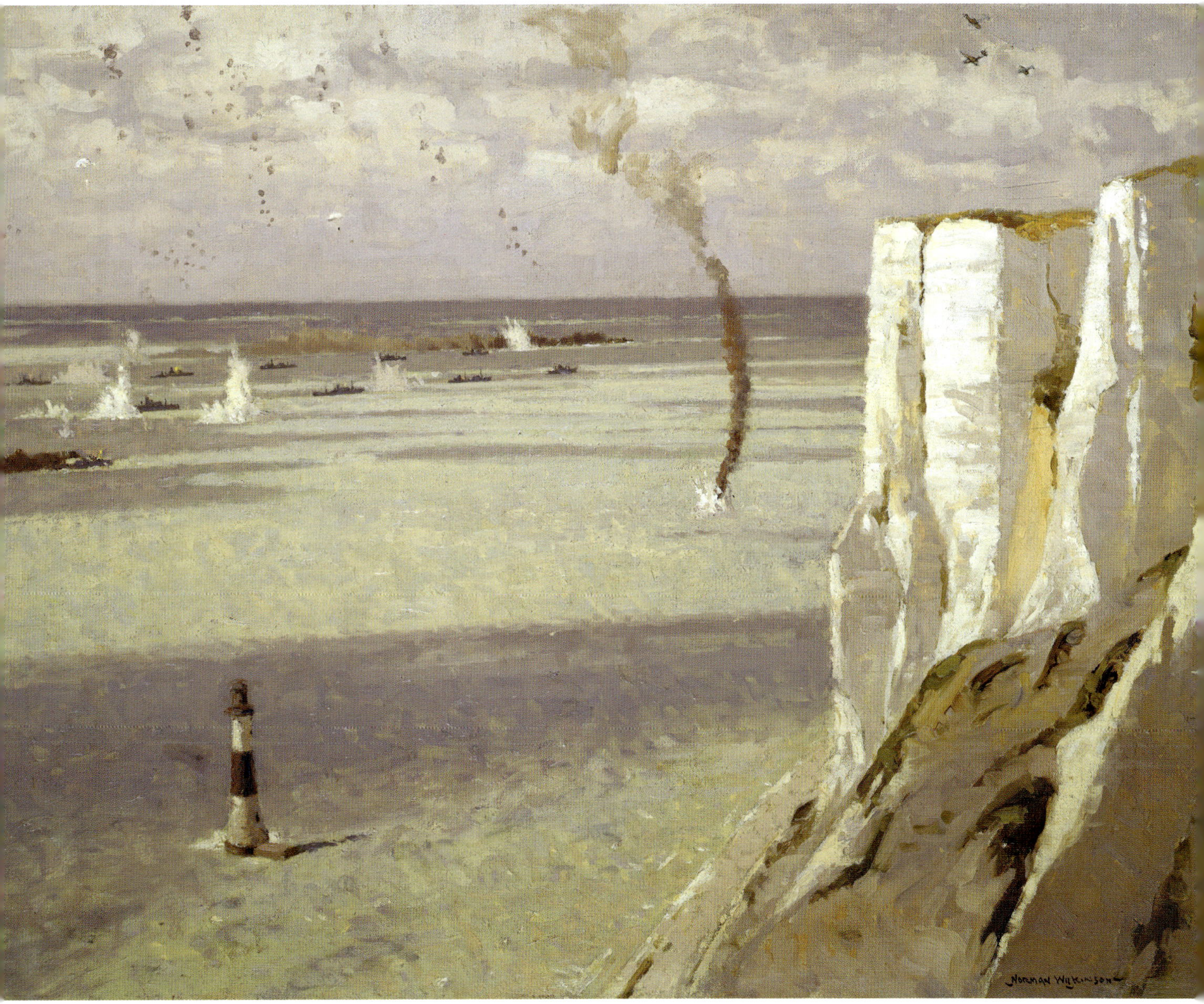

NORMAN WILKINSON
Beachy Head: Attack on Convoy
*c.*1942–4 | oil on canvas | 762 x 1016 mm

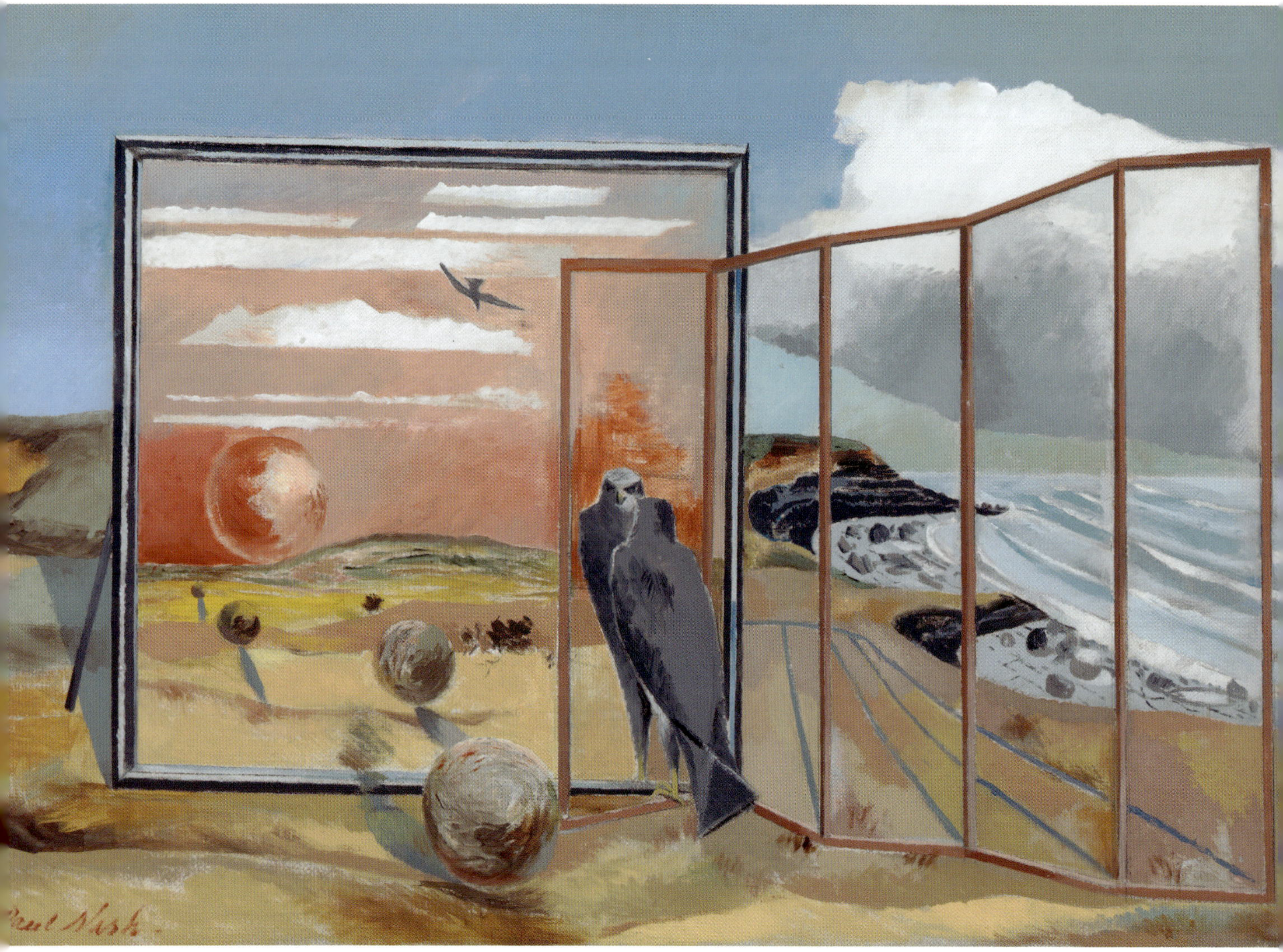

PAUL NASH
Landscape from a Dream
1936–8 | oil on canvas | 679 x 1016 mm

STRANGE TIDES

STEVE MARSHALL

FROM THE REASSURING SOLIDITY OF THE SHORE GENERATIONS of visitors have contemplated the sea: an altogether alien and often hostile environment, home to strange creatures and a gateway to exotic places. The shoreline is a meeting point for the opposing elements of earth and water, its intertidal zone not quite belonging to either. Here the bizarre detritus of the sea accumulates: the remains of unfamiliar animals and plants, flotsam and jetsam, the products of man and nature reshaped by the transformative power of the ocean. The constant attention of the waves fashions the landscape itself into the fantastic shapes of cliff, stack, arch and spit, ripping material from one place only to deposit it elsewhere. This environment has also been shaped by human intervention; the architecture and material culture of harbour and resort has a distinct identity, redolent of a maritime nation's exploitation of the coast's many opportunities for trade, travel and pleasure. It is not surprising then that during the twentieth century the south coast was to provide compelling subject matter for artists seeking to combine its dramatic landscape with an uncanny world of dreams and the unconscious mind.

The First World War had a profound impact on the art world. Pre-war modernist movements such as Futurism and Vorticism which had celebrated speed and machinery lost their glamour after the long years of mechanised slaughter and destruction. There was a return to more traditional, representational styles and in Britain many artists retreated to the countryside looking for reassurance in the peace and tranquillity of rural landscapes. It was not until the mid-1920s that they began to absorb new ideas emerging from the continent, principally surrealism and abstraction. The validity of these concepts and the question of how artists should respond to them came to be the primary topic for debate between artists and critics throughout the 1930s and 1940s.

The conflict between adherents of abstraction and those who preferred representation was to be particularly divisive. For Paul Nash (1889–1946) there was a question as to 'whether it is possible to "go modern" and still "be British"', in other words, to continue to respond to nature and the landscape in the British Romantic tradition.[1] The south coast was to play an important role for artists such as Nash and Ben Nicholson (1894–1982) as they tried to reconcile a desire to create something modern with their instinctive feeling for landscape.

1. Nash, P. (1932), 'Going Modern and Being British', in *Week End Review*, 12 March 1932, p.322.

Abstraction was a non-representational form of art, not intended to imitate visual reality but instead using form, colour and line to achieve its effect. Its supporters believed that since abstract art did not represent the real world it was therefore divorced from material things and a purer and potentially more spiritual art form. It was also promoted on the basis that it aligned with Plato's theories that the highest form of beauty lay not in nature but in geometry. Ben Nicholson visited the Paris studio of Piet Mondrian (1872–1944) in 1934 and was captivated by what he saw. When Mondrian later journeyed to London and visited Nicholson's studio in Hampstead he approved, but on seeing the view of a chestnut tree from the window chided 'too much nature.'[2] Nicholson's art quickly moved to a point where there was no concession to nature and, with his wife Barbara Hepworth, he developed a reputation for an uncompromising attitude towards the supremacy of abstraction over representation.

The French writer and poet André Breton (1896–1966) produced the *Manifesto of Surrealism* in 1924, stating that 'Surrealism is based in the belief in the superior reality of certain forms of association heretofore neglected, in the omnipotence of the dream, and in the disinterested play of thought.'[3] Breton's ideas were heavily influenced by Sigmund Freud's writings on the unconscious. The surrealists sought mechanisms to reveal the desires, emotions and memories repressed by the conscious mind, believing that true creativity stemmed from the unconscious. For Breton and his followers surrealism was more than an art movement, it was a way of life: Breton expected members of the group to rigorously adhere to its principles. However, in Britain there seems to have been a natural reluctance among artists to give themselves up to rigidly organised groups, and during the 1920s and 1930s most were more inclined to incorporate ideas which underpinned surrealism, rather than identify themselves as overtly surrealist artists.

In 1933 Paul Nash co-founded Unit One, a group of artists who stood 'for the expression of a truly contemporary spirit.'[4] The members included Henry Moore (1898–1986), Ben Nicholson, Barbara Hepworth (1903–75), Edward Wadsworth (1889–1949), Tristram Hillier (1905–83) and Edward Burra (1905–76). They held their first exhibition in London in 1934 which then toured the country, but by the beginning of the following year the group had disbanded. Despite Nash being Unit One's main champion his own interests seemed very much at odds with the group's declared purposes.[5] His challenge, and one that occupied him throughout the 1920s and 1930s, was how best to integrate ideas embodied in surrealism and abstraction into his own practice, while remaining true to his love of nature and preoccupation with the spirit of place. Two locations on the south coast were to play an important part in that process, Dymchurch and Swanage.

PAUL NASH FIRST VISITED DYMCHURCH ON THE KENT COAST in 1919 and was fascinated by the village's singular location, tucked behind a long sea wall that protected low-lying Romney Marsh from flooding. Two years later he and his wife Margaret decided to settle there and the wall was to become a recurring theme in his work over the next few years. Just prior to the move Nash had suffered a breakdown which was attributed to the trauma of his wartime service and the impact of losing a number of close friends both during and after the war. His almost obsessive focus on the sea wall has

2. Rothenstein, J. (1956), *Modern English Painters: Lewis to Moore*, Eyre and Spottiswoode, p.269.
3. Remy, M. (1999), *Surrealism in Britain*, Ashgate, p.18.
4. Nash, P., letter to *The Times*, 12 June 1933.
5. Haycock, D.B. (2002), *Paul Nash*, Tate Publishing, p.52.

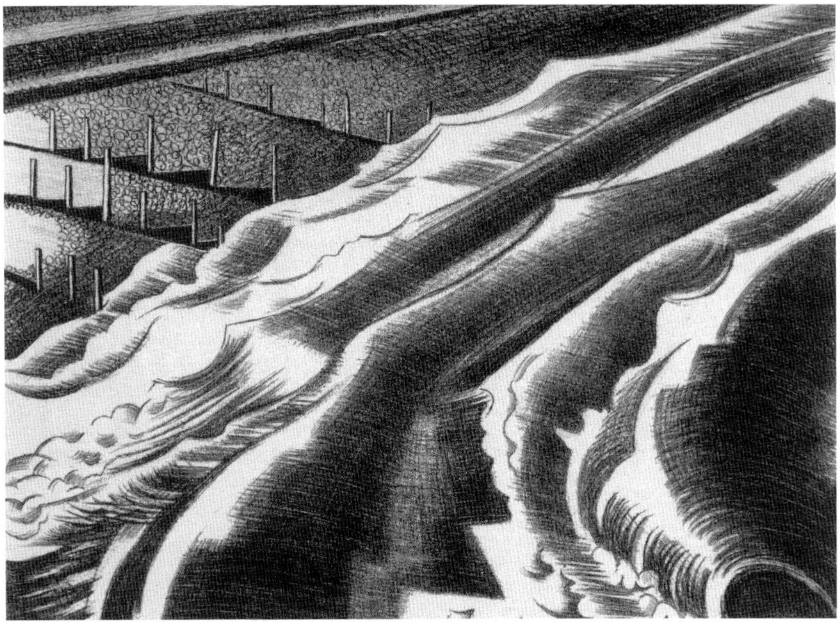

PAUL NASH
The Tide, Dymchurch
1920 | lithograph on paper | 314 x 422 mm
VICTORIA AND ALBERT MUSEUM.
GIVEN BY MRS MARGARET NASH, WIDOW OF THE ARTIST

been interpreted as a kind of catharsis, a working out of the psychological and emotional effects of his experiences in France and Belgium. Parallels have been drawn between the relentless battering of the sea against the man-made defences and the protective trench lines of the Western Front, where there was similarly no peace from the continual shelling, sniping and raiding.[6] It is a war of attrition between sea and land for which there will only be one winner.

There is undoubtedly a dark mood to *The Tide, Dymchurch* a lithograph produced in 1920 before the Nashes finally settled in the village. While he was recuperating from an injury sustained in the trenches in 1917, Nash had been introduced to lithography by fellow Slade-student Christopher Nevinson (1889–1946) who had been a keen supporter of Futurism.[7] Nash produced a series of powerful prints in the medium which were shown in the exhibition *Void of War* at the Leicester Galleries in 1918. *The Tide, Dymchurch* shares the dark and unsettling atmosphere of those wartime prints. Unusually in Nash's Dymchurch pictures, the view here is not from the wall itself but from a point over the water which serves to emphasise the power of the waves: the sea is infinite and remorseless while the defences built against it appear fragile and transient. The idea of a dangerous sea lapping at the English coast was to re-appear in one of Nash's most famous paintings of the Second World War. *Totes Meer (Dead Sea)* (1940–1), was painted after a visit to a dump for crashed German aircraft near Oxford, but Nash turned the mass of broken machines into waves threatening to inundate the land.

Nash was to find renewed inspiration on the south coast during the 1930s. For much of his life he was dogged by ill-health and from the mid-1930s

6. Causey, A. (2013), *Paul Nash: Landscape and the Life of Objects*, Lund Humphries, p.52.
7. Haycock, D.B. (2009), *A Crisis of Brilliance: Five Young British Artists and the Great War*, Old Street Publishing, p.275.

suffered a series of asthma attacks. In 1933, after a particularly difficult period, the Nashes were invited to stay with friends at Whitecliff farmhouse just to the north of Swanage. The following year they were loaned the property and with improving health Nash was able to revisit the world of his childhood holidays. In his unfinished autobiography Nash summarises this period as 'Blessed escape. Enchantment of the Ballard.'[8] At Whitecliff he worked on paintings of Avebury and the Dorset coast, finding ways to incorporate elements of surrealism and abstraction into landscapes that drew on the traditions of British Romantic art and poetry.

Nash had been given a camera by Margaret in 1931 and he used it avidly, capturing still-life images of objects such as fungi, stones and driftwood as well as elements in the landscape, both man-made and natural. While staying in Swanage he met and began an affair with the artist Eileen Agar (1899–1991), who was also to be closely associated with surrealism. They would spend hours together exploring the coast, collecting and photographing the strange objects they found there.[9] Nash had never been particularly comfortable in portraying human figures in his paintings but these discoveries gave him a cast of characters to include in his work as 'object personages'. He had found a means to marry nature and surrealism. Taking landscapes and found material with which he had forged particularly strong associations, he brought them together in strange juxtapositions that gave his paintings an uncanny and dream-like atmosphere. This was perfectly in line with the surrealists' desire to seek out and reveal the workings of the unconscious mind. *Voyage of the Fungus* (1936) shows fungi apparently rolling across the waves in Swanage Bay, *Circle of the Monoliths* (1938) transports stones from Avebury to the coast, hedges become breakwaters and the Pinnacle stack forms part of the stone circle out among the waves. *Event on the Downs* (1934) is based on the view of Ballard Down from Whitecliff and shows a tree stump and tennis ball placed together in the Dorset landscape. This has been interpreted as representing Nash's recently deceased father (after the First World War Nash seemed to have associated fallen trees and logs with the dead), the cloud above signifying the souls of the dead looking over the living, in this case the tennis ball possibly representing Nash himself.[10]

Nash's most famous rendering of the Dorset coast appears in the painting *Landscape from a Dream* (1936–8) (page 96) which was hailed by André Breton as a surrealist masterpiece. It is a bright day on the Purbeck coast, waves lap peacefully at the shore but a huge cloud looms on the horizon. On the downs above the cliffs a hawk perches on the frame of an empty screen gazing at its reflection in a mirror. The mirror is a window on another world where the sun is setting and another bird flies free before geometrically neat clouds. A sphere beside the hawk is also mirrored in the world beyond and similar objects are repeated, disappearing into the distance. The painting is open to many interpretations: mirrors can represent gateways into other worlds, perhaps in this case the afterlife with the spheres suggesting souls of the living and the dead. Nash owned an Egyptian figurine of a hawk, a symbol of Horus the sky god, and it has been suggested this stands for the artist.[11] The painting is a fine example of Nash using an identifiable English landscape as the setting for an uncanny assemblage of dream imagery and symbolism.

8. Nash, P. (1949), *Outline: An Autobiography*, Faber and Faber, p.187.
9. Denton, P. (2002), *Seaside Surrealism: Paul Nash in Swanage*, Peveril Press, p.10.
10. Causey, A. (2013), Op. cit., p.119.
11. Ibid., p.82.

Nash had enjoyed his time in Swanage and even considered building a house there, but he increasingly came to feel that it had been spoiled by development and the growing influx of tourists. He wrote an article for the *Architectural Review* in 1936 called 'Swanage, or Seaside Surrealism' which on the one hand celebrated the odd monuments and pieces of architectural salvage installed in the town by George Mowlem and George Burt, but also decried its current state: 'Modern Swanage is of such extreme ugliness, architecturally, that the inhabitants instinctively look out to sea or across the bay to the noble contour of Ballard Head.'[12] That year the Nashes departed for London.

EDWARD WADSWORTH HAD JOINED NASH AS A MEMBER OF Unit One in 1933. By this time he had become known for a series of tempera paintings based on groupings of maritime objects such as shells, sextants, compasses, floats, ship's logs and lights in bright coastal settings. Wadsworth had been a founder of the Vorticist group, an exhibitor at its London and New York exhibitions and a signatory to the manifesto published in the first issue of its journal *Blast* in July 1914. Vorticism was a British response to the ideas of Cubism and Futurism but its momentum was disrupted by the war and it had effectively fizzled out by 1919.[13] During the war Wadsworth used his experience of avant-garde geometry in Norman Wilkinson's Royal Navy Dazzle Camouflage Section.

In the summer of 1920 Wadsworth and his wife Fanny holidayed at Newlyn and although she was not impressed, writing in a letter 'Newlyn is a dull little hole and Cornwall not at all like the GWR posters,'[14] they were inspired to walk back to London along the south coast. The joys of walking twenty miles a day in poor weather wearing plimsolls and ordinary clothes had paled for Fanny by the time they reached Plymouth, but Wadsworth bought a pair of stout boots and completed the journey in the company of his dog 'X'. He decided that he would make a set of paintings emulating Turner's series on the ports and harbours of England, but while the project did not materialise he found new inspiration at Portland and Plymouth. Returning to Portland the following summer, Wadsworth produced several paintings of the area in watercolour and tempera including *Fortune's Well, Portland* (1921). These paintings focus on the regular geometry of houses, industrial buildings and chimneys but they are bordered by the natural curves of the surrounding coast and country. There is a continuity here with his pre-war work, particularly the woodcuts, which share the aerial perspective and reduction of buildings almost to a series of abstract shapes, all rendered with Wadsworth's precise draughtsmanship. It is easy to see how Fortuneswell's ranks of terraced houses made appealing subject matter for Wadsworth. Portland also held a romantic appeal for him, further stimulated by reading Thomas Hardy's novel *The Well-Beloved*, the story of a quarry owner's son who becomes a fashionable sculptor, and which features the little quarrying and fishing village in the guise of Street of Wells.[15]

If Wadsworth's paintings of Portland looked back to his pre-war style, then the paintings he produced after returning to Plymouth in 1922 and 1923 anticipated his work of the 1920s and 1930s. Wadsworth was particularly drawn to harbour scenes, revelling in the contrasts between the chaos of jumbled hulls and sails and the linear order of masts, rigging and dockside

12. Nash, P. (1936), 'Swanage, or Seaside Surrealism', *Architectural Review*, 79, April, pp.151–54.
13. Rylands, P. (2010), in *The Vorticists: Manifesto for a Modern World*, Tate Publishing, p.15.
14. Wadsworth, B. (1989), *Edward Wadsworth: A Painter's Life*, Michael Russell Publishing, p.95.
15. Ibid., p.95.

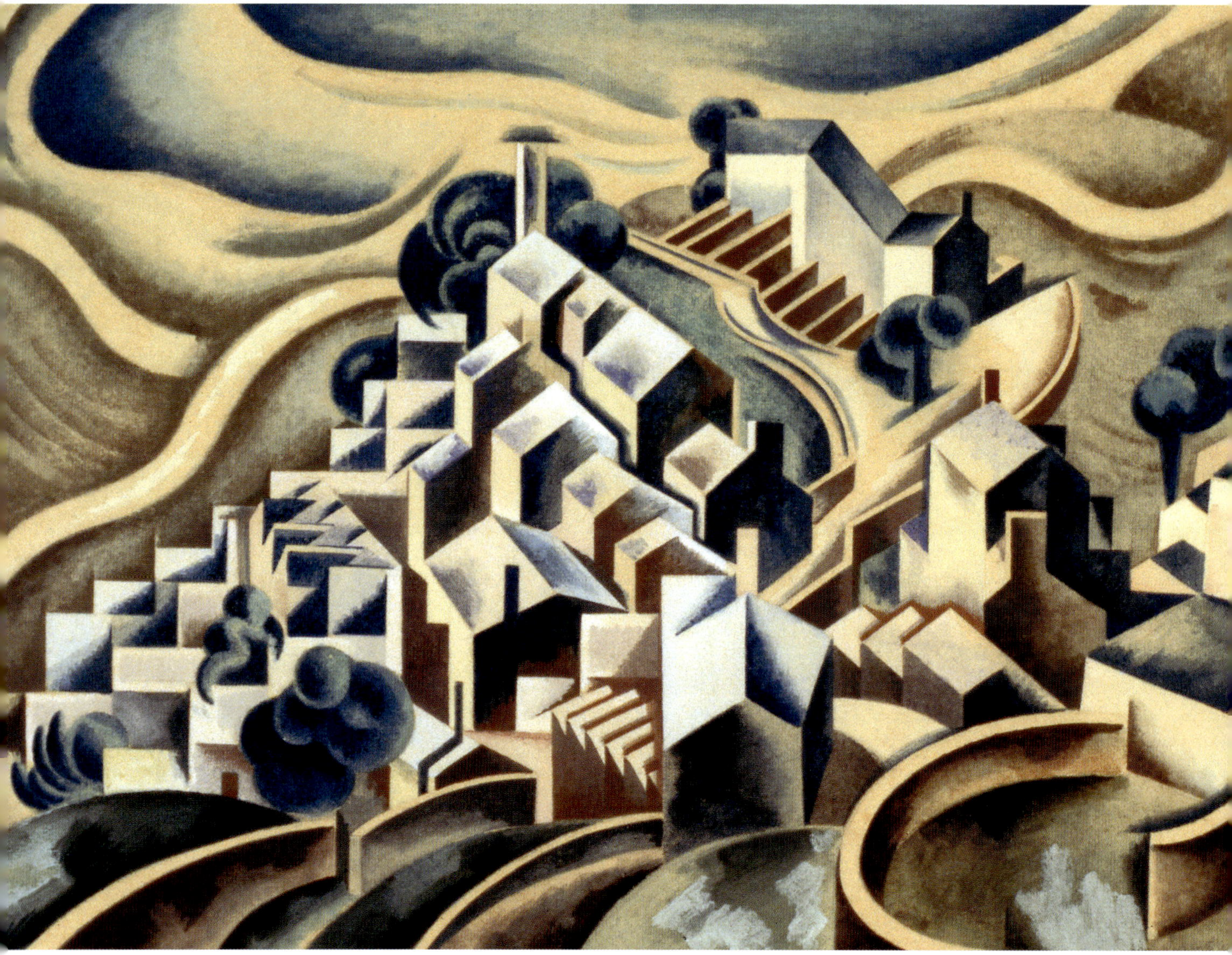

EDWARD WADSWORTH
Fortune's Well, Portland
1921 | watercolour | 552 x 795 mm

buildings. *The Cattewater, Plymouth Sound* (1923) was one of several new tempera paintings exhibited at the Leicester Galleries in 1923. It contrasts the sharp lines of the harbour wall with the curves of sailing boats and the hills and cliffs beyond, all portrayed in a slightly detached and dreamlike calm. *The Times* critic praised it for 'an austere and unsentimental beauty.'[16] A trip to the continent in 1923 was to have a major impact on the direction of Wadsworth's paintings. Harbour scenes at La Rochelle, Marseilles and St. Tropez continued the artistic journey begun at Plymouth, but by 1926 his subject matter was increasingly focused on assemblages of maritime objects set against a backdrop of harbour walls, beaches and placid seas. By taking objects out of their normal context, Wadsworth emphasised their inherent character and oddness, seemingly quite out of keeping with their intended purposes. Each item takes on a life of its own and appears strange and disconcerting. Wadsworth never saw himself as a surrealist but these uncanny paintings definitely share the movement's interest in dream imagery and the unconscious.[17]

BEN NICHOLSON AND BARBARA HEPWORTH WERE LIVING IN London just before the outbreak of the Second World War in August 1939. Concerned by the threat of air raids on the capital, they accepted an invitation from fellow artist Adrian Stokes (1902–72) to stay for a while at St. Ives. When it became clear that the war would not be over quickly they decided to settle there. Nicholson had developed a reputation as a pioneering modernist artist during the 1920s and 1930s, assimilating elements of cubism into still life paintings and creating his white reliefs informed by constructivist art's emphasis on process and materials. The landscape of the Cornish coast made an immediate impression on him and, in time, its influence was to find its way even into his most overtly abstract works.

Once established in Cornwall Nicholson continued to create white reliefs and abstract paintings, but he also began to make drawings and paintings of the landscape from his studio window and on trips around the coast. He made precise but spare drawings of farms and villages and was fascinated by the way the buildings seemed to be one with the windswept landscape. The remains of mine workings at Pendeen were the subject of a drawing that contrasted the sharp geometry of chimneys and engine houses with the lumpen contours of the post-industrial landscape.[18] The advent of war had a considerable impact on the art market and it became increasingly difficult to sell more challenging, abstract compositions. As money and materials were in short supply and dealers were looking for more saleable work, there may well have been a degree of pragmatism in Nicholson's decision to include landscape in his work,[19] but he does seem to have been genuinely compelled to assimilate the environment of the Cornish coast into his paintings while trying not to betray his modernist principles. In parallel with Paul Nash the solution lay in placing objects in a landscape setting.

Nicholson had been creating still life paintings since the 1920s which he developed using the multiple viewpoints and fractured geometry of cubism. In Cornwall the still life arrangements made a transition from a table in his studio to the windowsill, introducing the world beyond into the composition. *Still Life and Cornish Landscape* (1944) shows a plate, mugs, a jug and a cup set on a table before a window which opens on a view of High Carnstabba

16. Black, J. (2005), *Edward Wadsworth: Form, Feeling and Calculation*, Philip Wilson Publishers, p.53.
17. Remy, M. (1999), Op. cit., p.41.
18. Lewis, D. (1996), 'St. Ives: A Personal Memoir, 1947–55', in *St. Ives 1939–64: Twenty Five Years of Painting, Sculpture and Pottery*, Tate Gallery Publishing, revised edition, p.24.
19. Stephens, C. (2008), 'Ben Nicholson in Wartime', in *A Continuous Line: Ben Nicholson in England*, Tate Publishing, p.99.

Farm above St. Ives Bay.[20] *St. Ives Cornwall* (1943–5) placed the still life on a window sill with a view beyond of boats in the harbour which is reminiscent of Alfred Wallis. It was then perhaps a logical step to abandon the room and the window and place the still life directly into the landscape as in *November 11-47 (Mousehole)* (1947). The little harbour at Mousehole on Cornwall's Channel coast had been a popular subject for artists including Stanhope Forbes and Christopher Wood. Nicholson makes it the setting for a still life which floats like an apparition in the foreground. The patchwork fields are rendered in greens and yellows while the outlines of buildings and boats and the boundaries of the harbour are picked out in precise lines which are then echoed in the still life assemblage. This group might appear incongruous but Nicholson's careful handling of colour and texture binds the elements together. The colours of the still life are repeated in the landscape and the restricted palette brings calmness rather than menace to this odd juxtaposition. Exposure to the naive and nostalgic paintings of Alfred Wallis may, to a degree, have influenced Nicholson's approach to the Penwith landscape, but the natural environment of this rugged coast got under his skin. The still life in the landscape paintings are the most obvious expression of his feeling for place and he explained this quite simply in a letter to Patrick Heron in 1954: 'All the "still lifes" are in fact land-sea-sky scapes to me.'[21]

BEN NICHOLSON HAD INVITED JOHN TUNNARD (1900–71) TO join the Penwith Society in 1949 but he declined, preferring to pursue his own interests independent of outside influences. Tunnard and his wife Mary had arrived in Cornwall in 1930, settling at Cadgwith, a small fishing village on the Lizard peninsula. After leaving the Royal College of Art Tunnard had worked as a textile designer and once established in Cornwall they started a hand-block silk printing business. Early in his career Tunnard painted romantic landscapes, but during the 1930s he developed a highly individual style which was influenced by both surrealism and abstraction. He saw himself more as an abstract painter than a surrealist but he exhibited with the surrealists at the Artists International Association exhibition in 1937 and there are certainly echoes of the work of Joan Miró (1893–1983) and Yves Tanguy (1900–55) in Tunnard's compositions. He explained the development of his practice in an interview in 1944:

> I started certainly as a representational painter ... First, I suppose I was interested in merely trying to put down what I saw or thought I saw. Then, after that I was more interested in the dramatic content of the landscape ... and then ... with the geometrically dramatic content. By that I mean the dramatic movements of roads, of ruts sweeping into farmyards, of the lines of telegraph poles or the sweep of railings, and these I found myself exaggerating to get to the geometrically dramatic. Of course, I got to the stage when, confronted with a landscape, I felt that the only thing to do was invent. As soon as I started inventing I found that it was so much more exciting, and that inventing came gradually into what is called non-representational painting.[22]

Tunnard had an abiding interest in nature: landscape, geology, flora and even entomology (he collected specimens for the British Museum of Natural History and studied Kleidotoma subaptera, a type of parasitic wasp found among seaweed on the Cornish shore).[23] He also became fascinated by technology and all of these interests found their way into his work. The coastal

20. *St. Ives 1939–64: Twenty Five Years of Painting, Sculpture and Pottery*, Tate Gallery Publishing, revised edition 1996, p.170.
21. Letter from Ben Nicholson to Patrick Heron (February 1954) in Lewison, J. (1993), *Ben Nicholson*, Tate Gallery, p.86.
22. Glazebrook, M. (1977), 'Developments and Influences', in *John Tunnard 1900–1971*, Arts Council, p.22.
23. Glossop, R. (1977), 'A Personal Appreciation', in *John Tunnard 1900–1971*, Arts Council, p.8.

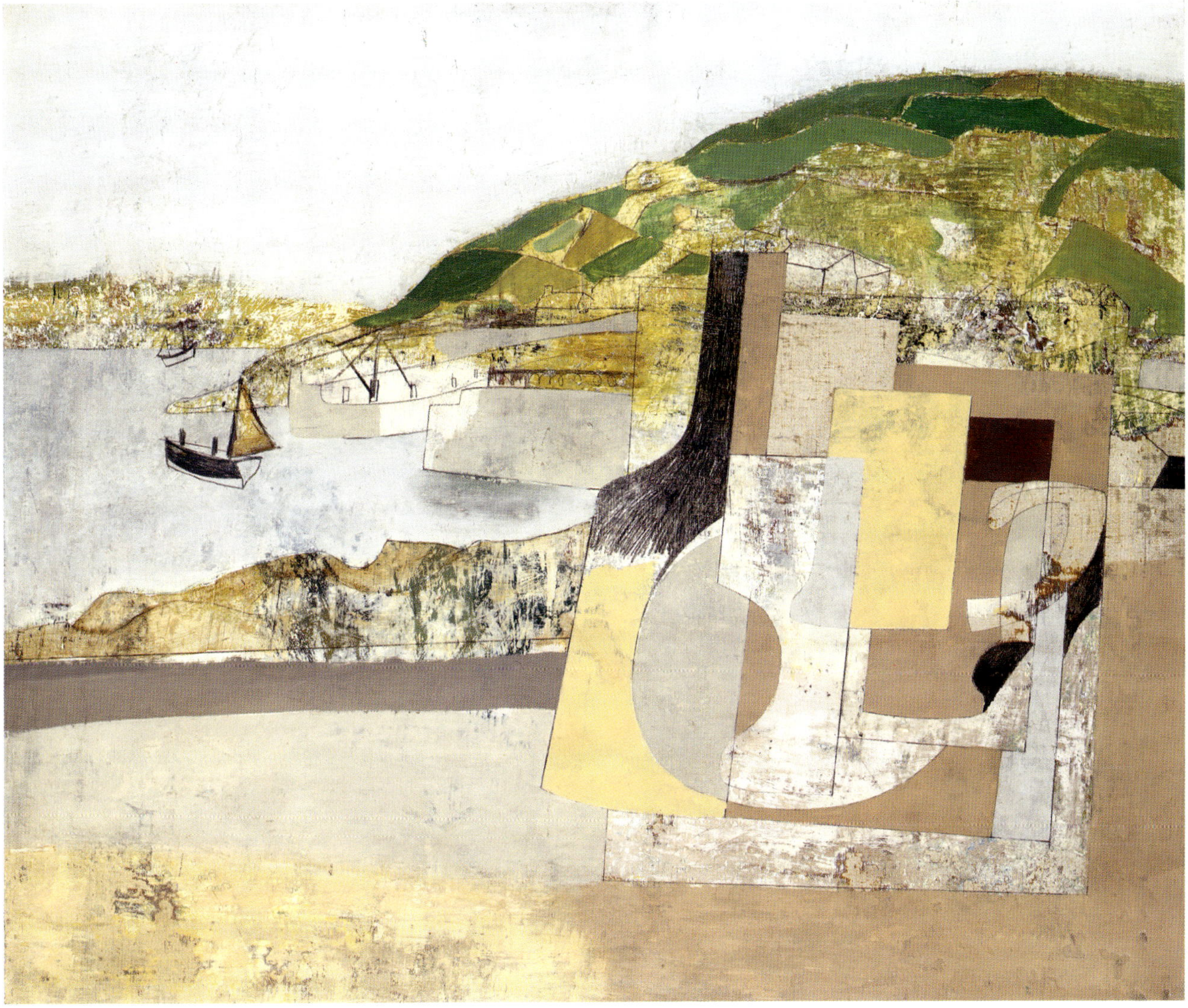

BEN NICHOLSON
November 11-47 (Mousehole)
1947 | oil on canvas | 465 x 585 mm

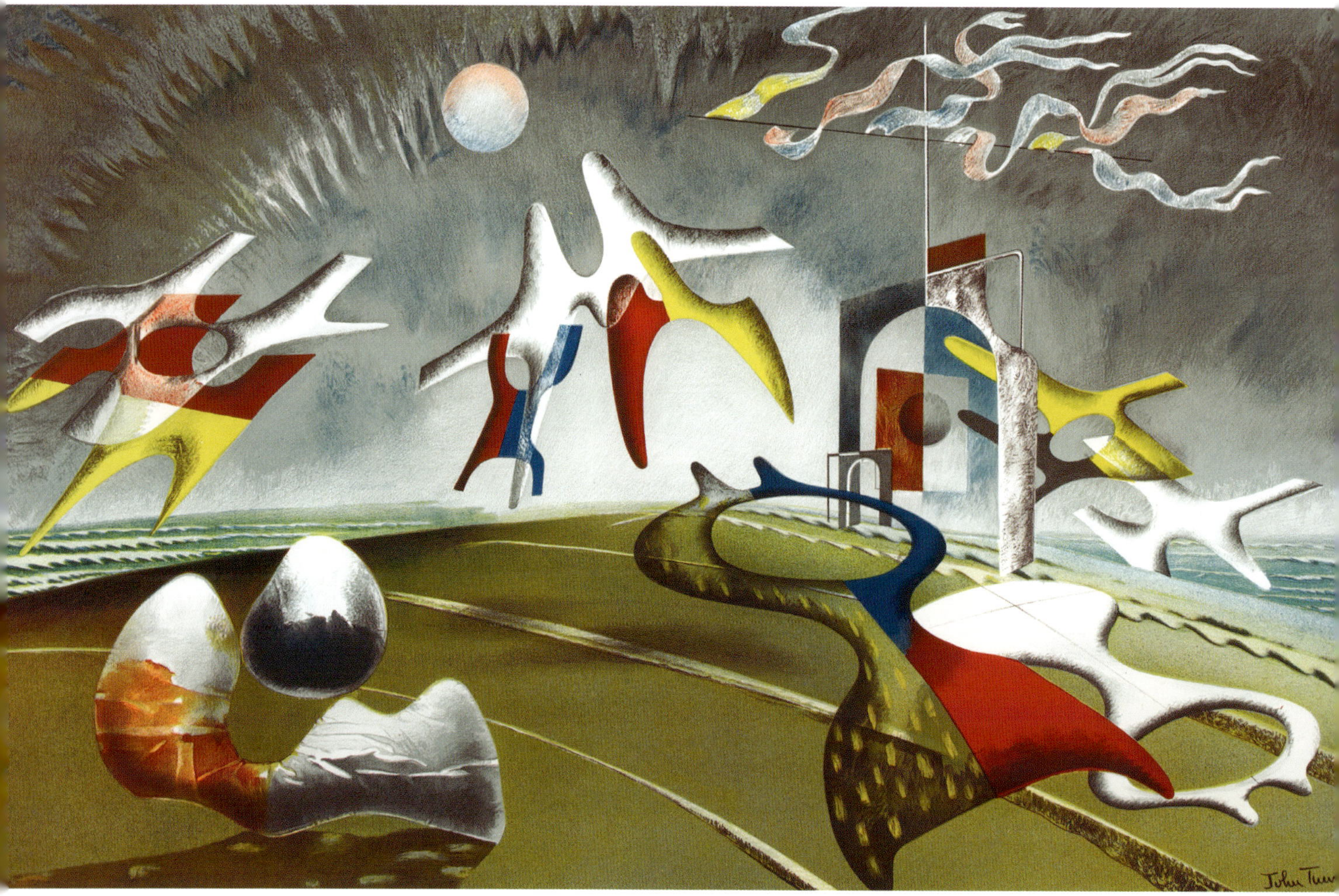

JOHN TUNNARD
Holiday
1947 | lithograph on paper | 495 x 762 mm

environment provided a context for his paintings; the Cornish cliffs, boats in a bay and waves breaking on the shore appear recognisably in works like *Clifftop Structure* (1938), but gradually these overt images of the natural world disappeared. Instead his paintings were dominated by intersecting planes and forms which drew on both machinery and nature but were recognisable as neither, figments instead of a strange inner world. He explained 'The objects you see in my paintings ... do in fact exist, but in a world of my own. This world of my own is just as natural to me as your world is to you, and possibly at some date you will encounter these shapes in your everyday experience.'[24]

Tunnard was a conscientious objector during the Second World War and served as an auxiliary coastguard, spending his days looking out to sea watching for German aircraft. He and Mary continued to make hand-block printed textiles, exchanging them for clothing coupons. Wartime and post-war austerity were difficult times for artists and it was probably under these straightened circumstances that Tunnard accepted a commission for the School Prints series of original artists' lithographs aimed at 'visual education' for primary schools. The School Prints selector Brenda Rawnsley had visited an exhibition of Tunnard's work at the Lefevre Gallery in London and asked if he might be interested in taking part.[25] Tunnard agreed and in return was to receive £85 plus a royalty of £10 per thousand prints sold to the public and £5 per thousand sold to schools.[26] *Holiday* (1947) was certainly the most abstract print produced, it was nevertheless very popular, probably due to its bright colours and the cheerful exuberance which it radiates. The figures may well be strange and surreal but they are by no means disconcerting and appear to be having a great deal of fun on a sunny beach as the waves roll in. *Holiday* was the only print which Tunnard ever produced.

AS AN ARTIST MONICA POOLE (1921–2003) SHARED TUNNARD'S interest in the minutiae of nature, although her chosen medium, the wood engraving, rooted her in a tradition for which surrealism and abstraction were rare influences. Poole was born in Canterbury and studied at the Thanet School of Art at Margate where she was introduced to wood engraving by Geoffrey Wales. Her education was interrupted by the war and factory work, but from 1945 she was able to study illustration at the Central School of Arts and Crafts, one of her tutors being the wood engraver John Farleigh. Despite a renaissance in the 1920s and 1930s, after the Second World War wood engraving became an unfashionable and somewhat forgotten medium, reserved mainly for book illustration. Poole, however, swam against this tide, only illustrating one book (*Kent* by Reginald Turnor, 1950) and concentrated instead on producing engravings on a larger scale intended to stand alone as artist's prints. She lived in Kent for most of her life and found her subject matter in its chalk downland, woods and rocky shores: 'It was the material for a visual language of chastening austerity and cool, sub-lunar richness, bordering at times on the surreal.'[27] Poole's fascination with lifeless rock forms and dead trees has been interpreted as stemming from personal battles with illness, depression and bereavement and her friend and fellow wood engraver George Mackley commented that her work 'moved far from the purely perceptual into the strongly conceptual.'[28]

The striking forms of rocks, clouds and driftwood in Poole's prints reflect the influence of Henry Moore and John Minton (1917–57) and she spoke of being

24. Peat, A. and Whitton, B.A. (1997), *John Tunnard: His Life and Work*, Scolar Press, p.85.
25. Artmonsky, R. (2010) *The School Prints: A Romantic Project*, Artmonsky Arts, p.36.
26. Peat, A. and Whitton, B.A. (1997) Op. cit., p.86.
27. Brett, S. (2003), 'Monica Poole 1921–2003: A Tribute', in *The Society of Wood Engravers*, Society of Wood Engravers, p.76.
28. Jaffé, P. (1990), *Women Engravers*, Virago, p.90.

particularly moved by the tree-forms of Graham Sutherland (1903–80).[29] *Driftwood* (1979) captures both the drama of the wider coastal landscape with the microcosm of the intertidal zone. The foreground is populated with stones and driftwood rounded by the sea into strange forms that would not be out of place in a Tunnard composition. Repeating patterns of rocks recede towards the distant cliffs while in the sky there hangs a menacing shape like a giant winged creature about to shatter the almost oppressive stillness below. *Edge of the Sea* (1972) shows the tide running in among faceted rocks which are the home to limpets and barnacles, although even these creatures show no signs of life and seem simply to be extensions of the rocks to which they cling. *Piddock Architecture* (1975) is a prime example of Poole's interest in the inherent strangeness of natural forms, here she focuses on a single piece of rock in which holes have been made by the burrowing of Pholadidae or piddocks, a type of bivalve. Poole's engravings are marked by incredibly fine lines and hatching which provide a wide range of tones, there are spaces of pure white but very few areas of solid black. As a result there is an intensity of lighting that serves to heighten the strange atmosphere of her compositions.[30] Poole may not have seen herself as a follower of Nash, Wadsworth or Tunnard but she was similarly inspired by the strangeness she encountered on the margins of the coast, and in that sense part of a peculiarly English obsession with the uncanny possibilities of the Channel shore.

29. Fenwick, S., 'Monica Poole: Obituary', in *The Guardian*, 13 August 2003.
30. Hamilton, J. (1994), *Wood Engraving and the Woodcut in Britain c.1890–1990*, Barrie & Jenkins, p.151.

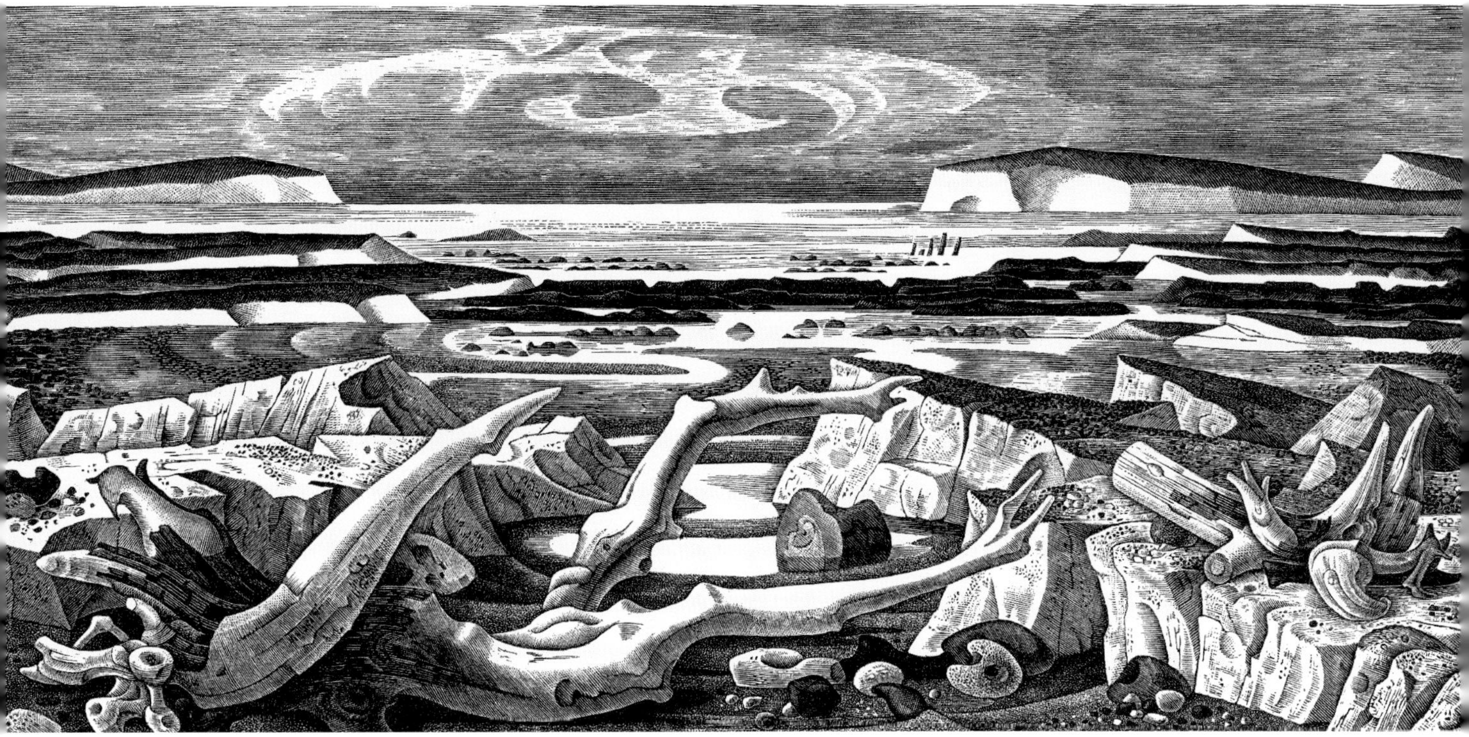

MONICA POOLE
Driftwood
1979 | wood engraving | 125 x 278 mm

INDEX

ABOUT THE AUTHORS

GILL CLARKE is Guest Curator at St. Barbe Museum & Art Gallery, Lymington where most recently she curated with Steve Marshall 'Home Lad, Home: The War Horse Story'. She is also Visiting Professor at the University of Chichester's Otter Gallery where she curated 'From Fields to Factories: Women's Work on the Home Front in the First World War'. Her books include *Randolph Schwabe: A Life in Art* (2012), *The Women's Land Army: A Portrait* (2008) and *Evelyn Dunbar: War and Country* (2006) all published by Sansom & Co.

STEVE MARSHALL is Exhibitions Curator and former Director of St. Barbe Museum & Art Gallery, where he has curated a number of exhibitions on British marine painting and individual artists including William Gilpin, Thomas Rowlandson, Sven Berlin and Richard Eurich. He has also recently curated the exhibition 'The Artists Rifles: from Pre-Raphaelites to Passchendaele' for Southampton City Art Gallery and Hampshire Cultural Trust and was a contributor to Kurt Jackson's Place project.